WHY THEY FOLLOW

How to Lead with Positive Influence

Scott Love

Copyright © 2016 by Scott Love
All rights reserved.

ISBN: 1518650295
ISBN 13: 9781518650291
Library of Congress Control Number: 2015919393
CreateSpace Independent Publishing Platform
North Charleston, South Carolina

TABLE OF CONTENTS

Introduction		v
About The Author		vii
Chapter 1	Your Power to Influence	1
Chapter 2	Three Steps to Servant Leadership	5
Chapter 3	Building Influence with Vision	9
Chapter 4	A Positive Alternative to Constructive Criticism	13
Chapter 5	Joel Parker	16
Chapter 6	Better Influence with Balance	19
Chapter 7	Mostly Give	22
Chapter 8	Improving Team Accountability	25
Chapter 9	Becoming "Followable"	29
Chapter 10	Follow Your Minesweeper	33
Chapter 11	Positive Influence in Times of Bad news	37
Chapter 12	Show How Their Work Matters	40
Chapter 13	Catalyst Management	43
Chapter 14	Changing the Culture of a Company	46
Chapter 15	The Chronic Complainer	49

Chapter 16	Clarify Expectations With New Employees	52
Chapter 17	Clarifying Core Values	55
Chapter 18	Cleaning Up Someone Else's Mess	58
Chapter 19	Conflict Resolution: A New Approach	61
Chapter 20	Leadership Development on a Budget	64
Chapter 21	Focus on the Personal Benefit	68
Chapter 22	The Four M's of Performance Improvement	71
Chapter 23	Giving Control to the Team	75
Chapter 24	Hiring Your Customer	78
Chapter 25	Take Advantage of Your Advantage	81
Chapter 26	How to Influence Self-Motivation	85
Chapter 27	How to Earn High Marks as a Leader	88
Chapter 28	How to Fill Critical Positions	92
Chapter 29	How to Listen with Positive Influence	96
Chapter 30	Investing in Employees	99
Chapter 31	Authenticity to Influence Sales	103
Chapter 32	Strategic Influence on Employees	106
Chapter 33	Leadership Styles	109
Chapter 34	Leadership by Question-Asking	112
Chapter 35	Positive Influence in Critical Situations	114
Chapter 36	The Problems with Command and Control	119
Chapter 37	Influencing in Times of Chaos	122
Chapter 38	Mission Accomplishment	126

INTRODUCTION

Why do most people purchase leadership books? Because they want to become a better leader. What exactly does that mean? It means that they will move to a place that I call "followable".

Whenever you are in a leadership role and when you give a directive, people have a choice in how they respond. They have a choice in how much enthusiasm they bring to the equation in the execution of your directive. On a scale of one to ten, with ten meaning they are most enthusiastic in their compliance, they are choosing how much energy and commitment they will contribute to achieving this goal.

I've seen sailors respond with a one to the captain and a ten to a junior officer, all because of the personal leadership shown by the person leading the way. I've seen line-level peers lead in a way that inspires the rest of the team and I've also seen chairmen of international organizations conduct themselves in a way that instills fear and alarm, resulting in a leadership response that is at the bottom of the compliance commitment range.

It doesn't matter your title or status in the company. What matters is how you lead.

Why *do* they follow?

If you want to derive better outcomes as a leader, then you first need to understand why people follow.

When I first considered writing this book and came up with the name and conducted research, I was surprised that nobody else had claimed it. I believe in simplicity, and the easiest and most effective way to bring people over the arc from ineffective to high performing leadership is to teach them why people follow. There are different ways to teach leadership. It is a concept that, no matter your age or level of seniority in an organization, requires continued study and discussion. I believe that the most effective way to teach leadership, with the exception of actually doing it, is to learn through stories. As I compiled the best stories and essays from my collection to help you learn, I kept that question in my mind. Why do they follow?

I hope that my stories inspire you to lead in a way that is in alignment with the hearts and minds of your colleagues, peers, and employees.

Scott T. Love

ABOUT THE AUTHOR

Scott Love is an expert on influence and persuasion. With more than two decades of C-Suite sales experience, he brings battle-tested leadership and sales solutions to executives, managers, leaders and sales people.

In his business presentations, Scott delivers a life-changing message with concrete action steps that helps managers and sales people gain more influence with and compliance from prospective customers, clients, employees and colleagues. This results in a boost in sales and helps employees maximize their performance. He is a popular speaker at sales meetings, business conferences and trade association conventions.

Scott has been quoted in the Wall Street Journal, Selling Power Magazine, and dozens of business publications and trade journals around the globe. He is a graduate of the United States Naval Academy in Annapolis, Maryland, and is married with two children and one hamster. His other business interests include consulting to companies on leadership and sales issues, speaking at sales meetings and business conventions, and working as a high-stakes headhunter for Washington law firms. In DC he is known as "Washington's legal power broker."

Visit his website for free tools and videos on the topic of influence: www.scottlove.com.

CHAPTER 1
YOUR POWER TO INFLUENCE

I spent the last few days of my vacation with a relative during his last few days, at a hospice home. The home was a lovely and peaceful setting for its guests and visitors - all except for the neighboring building next door. I was enraged the first time I heard how loud they were. Don't they know that people are grieving over here? How dare they! The noisy white Montessori school was within earshot of the hospice home and only a few yards away. The children laughed and screamed loudly without a single piece of quiet respect as they swallowed up the playground in a melee of activity. Couldn't the teaching staff show some courtesy by at least trying to keep the noise down?

I was curious at how all the windows and doors of the hospice home were propped open, especially those that were facing the Montessori school. Then I saw that even some guests were sitting outside of their rooms, quietly listening to the playful children.

And then I realized what was going on. The playful sounds emanating from next door were not damaging but nurturing. Either through divine intervention or bad zoning, the relationship between these two facilities grew into a balance of healing and harmony, with the Montessori school doling out generous doses of energy and power to the guests in the hospice home.

We all affect each other in our relationships, especially at work. Each day you bring with you a potential to affect other people. You bring the potential to create synergistic and symbiotic harmony, whether you know it or not. As a leader, you need to concern yourself with how you impact others. Sometimes the things that you say or do to your co-workers moves them in ways not obvious. You may not even realize it. Your influence has power.

Recently I was visiting with a friend who had just left her employer. She told me how her manager rarely said positive comments to his staff, but when he did it was only in private in his office. The time that he spent on the floor of the factory was spent complaining about his employees, publicly bringing attention to their faults in front of their peers. She was devastated, humiliated, and demoralized. "He never knew how much he influenced all of us, and never understood how damaging his influence was. And now he wonders why morale is so bad over there."

If you supervise or manage even one or two co-workers, then you have been given a heavy responsibility, and the responsibility for the morale of this team sits squarely on your shoulders. Here are three ways to develop positive feelings and improve the mood and morale of your staff.

1. **Catch people doing something right and bring it to their attention.** It can be a spontaneous and verbal recognition of their effort, or you can do it through an annual awards banquet or a quarterly function that recognizes performance and achievement. Either way, you can harness the power of social influence to shape the premises of what is accepted as strong performance. If your organization has the ability, put these awards and stories in a newsletter or mp3 format to distribute to employees. Interview or make recordings of these team members who have earned the recognition because of their performance speak for themselves, sharing what they did to receive the award. This doubles as a training moment, and also inspires co-workers to stretch beyond their reach.
2. **Keep a positive and optimistic outlook.** Your mood is the thermostat of the team's attitude, and everyone looks to you to see how you to gauge it. If you face a grave circumstance within your company, stay encouraging and offer hope with empathy to your colleagues and co-workers. Hope exists in everything. It's up to you to find that hope and share it with everyone else.
3. **Understand how much power your influence really carries.** An arrogant rolling of the eyes, a careless word, and a rude remark can point your team in the direction of apathy. Each contact that you have

with a member of your team will either add to or take away from the interdependent nature of your relationship.

The entire culture of your organization can be shaped and molded through the power of your influence that you wield as a leader. Take care to influence it in a positive manner.

CHAPTER 2
THREE STEPS TO SERVANT LEADERSHIP

When I was a first-year midshipman at Annapolis, I was surprised to hear combat veteran Marine Corps and Naval officers share how leadership is servanthood. I always had the impression that leadership was more of a glorious task of getting a chest full of medals. But the real core of leadership is about being an unglamorous servant. Marine Corps officers are always the last to eat when in the field. Leadership is about putting the needs of others ahead of yourself. Serving others, as long as it is in the direction of achieving your corporate goals, is the true essence of effective leadership. Leadership is about seeking out what motivates a subordinate, and figuring out how that internal motivation can be harnessed to help the team achieve its goals, thereby giving a sense of personal achievement to that employee.

The only problem with all this is that the task of having a servant's heart goes in the opposite direction of our human nature. But there is a simple process to real personal change on a transformational level. If an executive chooses not to change and grow in this way, then he will not be considered "followable" by his employees. If he is not followable, then his team will only go through the motions of their tasks, leading to mediocre results. A real leader must be worthy of having followers, and that, more than anything, is a character issue.

Leadership is more of a matter of what you are, not what you do.

Many executives of today are seeking their leadership solutions in short term quick fix tricks and tactics. If I push this button, I'll get this response. If I just say things this way, I can manipulate my people into following me to help me reach my goals. Short sighted thinking can only work well on a short term basis. Short term methods do not build long term trust between the leader and his follower.

There are three steps to growing in character and developing a heart that is worthy of being followed. It doesn't matter whether you are an executive, a secretary, a production manager, a sales representative, an engineer, a schoolteacher, or a homemaker.

Everyone is a leader.

Everyone influences others and is influenced by them. If you are even a first-year college student starting at the bottom of the organization, you must still assume the heart of leadership and grow in that area. And as you do, if you are faithful in those little items of team leadership, you will be rewarded and given greater levels of responsibility.

1. **Have a prosperous heart.** A prosperous heart believes that there is room in the organization for everyone to achieve satisfaction. Everyone can achieve the victory when the team does. By ensuring that every single person in the organization wins when the company wins, then you increase the probability of success of the team achieving its goals. A prosperous heart does not hold the glory for itself. Rather, at the end of the day, the leader with the prosperous heart appears invisible to the team. A successful leader will have his team members carrying on about how they accomplished the tasks themselves.
2. **Live in a way that is congruent with your heart.** What that means is that you need to clearly identify those values and principles which guide the way you do business and live your life. Once you have identified those, you can develop a certain sort of code. In the boy scouts, they call it the Scout Oath. In the military they have a code of conduct. Many professions have some sort of oath or ceremony to dedicate their newly indoctrinated members into a commitment toward a higher calling. Once that calling has been identified, you can start making

clear decisions within the framework of that calling or code.
3. **Communicate this trust to your staff.** Because you are living in a predictable sort of way in alignment with your heart or code or values, others around you will see this commitment. If you are in a supervisory position, you need to articulate the values of your group in some sort of fashion. By communicating the spirit of your unit to your team, you are creating silent accountability. People who believe in the team will actually start following your very own commitment to those same values and principles. By having a unified team whose heart is beating in the same way, trust begins to develop. This trust is a byproduct of the personal transformation that you personally develop. Leadership is a very personal issue, and cannot be institutionalized. The true measure of success as a leader is the amount of trust and commitment that he gains from his fellow teammates.

Many new managers will be surprised at the simplicity of leadership. That's because leadership is more of an issue of character rather than of competence. It is still an issue of competence, but more of the key measurements of leadership are focused on character-related issues. By taking these first three steps to developing a heart for leadership, you will have others around you take notice, and begin to see over time how they trust you more, are influenced by you, and are more willing to commit to you and to your cause.

CHAPTER 3
BUILDING INFLUENCE WITH VISION

"Our firm's growth was twenty-five percent last year, and I'm still feeling frustrated," he said. He was a new client of mine, running a $30 Million a year fee-based professional services firm in San Francisco. His frustration wasn't based on a monetary or a revenue issue. It was based on performance issues. To his competitors, his amazing growth was enviable. But he knew his staff wasn't performing at their peak levels. In fact, they were mediocre. "How can I motivate my staff to give 100 percent throughout the whole day?"

"Let's talk about that, Bob. Let's start with why your company exists. What is your company's purpose?"

"Well…" he said with careful thought, "to generate profits for me and my partners." I could tell by his hesitation and the answer he gave that had never really addressed this fundamental issue.

"So what you're telling me is that your sole purpose of what your company does is based on your personal profit and the profits of your key partners. Am I understanding you correctly?" I asked in my challenging style as the "tough love" management consultant.

"Yeah. That's it, I suppose. Our purpose is to decrease our costs, build up our revenues, and expand my net profits."

"That's your problem, Bob. It's a blah blah blah purpose that really misses the mark of what a company is all about. You haven't even mentioned the impact of your contribution to the world or what sort of value you create. If you fixate your purpose on profit margins or revenue, then you'll eventually fail. If you focus on the contribution to others who can benefit from your service, then the profits will take care of themselves."

To build a company or any well-functioning organization, first you start with building a purpose. Forget about making a profit. Instead, make a difference. When I do sales training I tell the sales reps that if they focus first on their contribution and not on the commissions, that they'll generate more commissions. The purpose of your organization has to be rooted in a fundamental resolution of an issue that can benefit some other person or organization significantly. In this increasingly competitive market, the difference that you make in the world is what makes the difference in your business. And when it comes to building and managing a motivated workforce, keep in mind that everyone wants to make a difference. Profit generation is a byproduct of a solid and crystal clear purpose. At the end of the day, your employees want to know that their work matters and when they know that it does, they will give it their all.

So here's the question you need to bring to your next staff meeting, the same question that I asked my client in California:

"What is the purpose of our organization?"

Think in terms of the contribution that you make to your customer. Focus on a tangible benefit felt on a personal level to the end user. Commit it to memory. Create a short paragraph of a mission statement or a purpose statement. Train everyone in your company on what that purpose is, and by all means, seek their input when you develop this statement of mission. This purpose cannot be self-serving, self-seeking, or related to the growth of your company. It must be external if your organization's success is measured in terms of serving an external entity.

A few years ago I was talking with a construction superintendent of a major school construction project. "What motivates you to build this school when you feel the pressure of the deadlines and other forces outside of your control?" I asked him. He told me that he wasn't just building a school. He was building a crucible for the hope of the future. His motivation was intrinsic and came from within. He had a clear understanding of his purpose and mission at work and he was a highly motivated employee, all because of his crystal clear focus on his contribution and purpose.

The difference between a high performing organization and one that just performs at a minimal level is the difference that your leadership can make by helping your employees understand why they come to work every day.

CHAPTER 4
A POSITIVE ALTERNATIVE TO CONSTRUCTIVE CRITICISM

Constructive criticism is a myth. If it really worked then we'd all be perfect by now.

Remember when someone gave constructive criticism to you? Were you motivated to improve and take their advice or was it just plain awful and you couldn't wait for that moment to end? The motive was probably well intentioned by the person that wanted to help you overcome your deficit, but the method of delivery usually ends up developing into a deficit itself.

Consider how you give constructive criticism to your employees when you see an area in them that needs to be improved. "Why can't they just take my advice?" you ask yourself when you give feedback to them. You might not visibly see the harm in how you do it, but the veiled and valid emotions that swell up in your subordinates' hearts will cloud their perspective. The feelings of anger, self-doubt, and insecurity overpower and overshadow any logical desire to improve. The result is a frustrated employee, a frustrated manager, and a deficit that still needs fixing.

So how can we as managers communicate with our employees in a way that gets the point across without getting them angry? How can we get them to see their areas of weakness and instill within them a desire to improve? To find the answer, I went straight to the source. Dr. Kenneth Christian is the author of *Your Own Worst Enemy: Breaking the Habit of Adult Underachievement* and the founder of the Maximum Potential Project (www.maxpotential.com). I asked Dr. Christian, a corporate management consultant and former practicing psychologist, the best way that a manager can help an employee overcome a deficit. In other words, what is the model of a "tough love" conversation that a manager can follow when a performance issue needs to be addressed?

First, he says, develop the approach. Tell your employee that your motive is to develop him and to take him to a new level in his career. Try saying something like "I want to take you somewhere you haven't been before in terms of your performance. If I could work with you and we could help you to get to a whole other level, would you explore working with me on (area of deficit) and see how far you could go?"

Second, reaffirm the confidence that you have in them. Dr. Christian says to tell your employees that you see something special in them, something that is above normal. Tell them this: "I know you can go farther and that you hold a strong presence of future success. I want to help you get there."

Third, work with them in appraising their strengths. Ask them the questions that cause them to find out what it is that causes them to excel. Specifically, what is their value as a member of your team? Why are they able to perform well in certain key areas? Then move to the "soft spots" in their performance. Specifically, what are those areas that need improvement? Ask them the questions and let them tell you. People usually are cognizant of their weaknesses. By being the leader they can trust, they can admit them to you and together you come up with a plan of overcoming them.

Finally, Dr. Christian says that you need to help them leave behind that old identity that they have of themselves and introduce them to the new identity of stronger performance. Include a big upside of what happens when they reach that new level of performance. Help them become comfortable with their success. Be very clear and specific about the upside benefit of this new level of performance to help increase their motivation to achieve at that level.

By following this model of thought and communication, you will build trust, develop a commitment to improve, and most importantly create a safe place to discuss areas of weakness. Your employees may never become perfect, but at least they'll take ownership of their weaknesses and will eagerly embrace a plan for improvement.

CHAPTER 5
JOEL PARKER

You've probably never heard of Joel Parker. He is a successful young entrepreneur and has figured out the keys to successful sales and customer service at such a young age. With only six years of business experience, he has learned the following:

1. **Identify the needs of your customer before you pitch your product or service to them.** Joel understands that his purpose is to solve a personal problem for his customers, and to serve them in an emotional capacity. He knows that his customers make decisions based on emotional reasons, not intellectual ones. So when he makes first contact with them, he addresses the benefit of his service, not his service. He explains to his prospects how his service can benefit them on a personal level, and this appeals to their emotions. As a result, his customers usually end up

saying 'thank you' to him at the conclusion of the transaction.

2. **Approach your customers with confidence and respect by developing a legitimate relationship with them.** Joel never gets too close to his customers until he feels the relationship is developing at the proper pace. He never rushes the relationship, but lets it build to the point that serves his customers. He maintains appropriate distance and respect, but still is engaging and respectful. His sincere interest in them is what attracts them to him. And when you meet him, you know that he is sincere. Joel knows that self-serving manipulation is a turn-off in his competitive industry, and recognizes that his prospects can intuitively sense it.

3. **Identify patterns of buying behavior of previous customers, and use that to guide you in your marketing efforts.** Don't 'profile' your prospects based on appearance but rather qualify them based on the criteria of those in the past that have bought from you. Identify the characteristics of those previously satisfied customers, and use that as the guiding criteria in finding future prospects. Don't consider appearance or dress. In Joel's business, he has learned that those prospects who are best suited to benefit from his service are sometimes the most poorly dressed. He doesn't let appearance qualify or disqualify those who he tries to serve. Instead, he finds the ones who have the highest probability of benefiting from his service, and puts the odds in his favor

by targeting the group most likely to buy based on circumstance and situation and not appearance.
4. **Don't let the negative jealousy of your competitors drag you down.** In Joel's business, he is the envy of his competitors. Many have said that his success stems from luck and chance, but Joel knows better. He knows that it is the attitude of giving to others and seeking ways to serve them that has caused him to become successful in his business.
5. **Target your repeat customers, and make it easy for them to buy from you over and over.** Joel has developed a broad client base, and goes well beyond what many of his competitors would do. He earns more than his competitors, but that's because of the amount of contribution he makes in the lives of his loyal customer base.
6. **Have fun at what you do.** Joel is completely fulfilled with his business and loves every minute of every day. It is this engaging work that compels him to succeed, and gives him an edge over his competitors.

By the way, if you are ever in Phoenix, you can find Joel at the baggage claim area in Terminal Four. He is a skycap and one of the more successful ones in his company. I met Joel several years ago in Phoenix on the way to a speaking engagement. I asked him what separated him from all the other skycaps, and what I received was a short lesson on business success. Principles of success in business never change, whether you are selling microchips, hotel rooms, or moving luggage from baggage claim to the trunk of a car.

CHAPTER 6
BETTER INFLUENCE WITH BALANCE

His nervous twitch wouldn't go away. It bothered me in our meeting and I tried not to look at it but couldn't help it. This was one tense CEO and it showed. He was stretched well beyond his limits and seemed to have surrendered to the challenges of running a large organization. His entire life was spent responding from one crisis to another.

I could empathize with him because I've been there, too. Living on reactive fumes instead of a proactive tank of gas is a problem with most executives and managers. They have too much on their plate. They must react to their immediate issues and cannot take the time out of their busy day to think strategically. Many managers understand how important it is to build up the systems and processes of a company, but if they take the time to do that, then their deadlines are missed and their current opportunities are gone forever or given to a competitor.

The more time you spend in the strategic focus and direction of your company, then the easier it is to run it. But how can you become strategic when most of your time is spent on tactical issues?

Consider these three steps to balancing your workday between the strategic and tactical issues that compete for your time:

1. **Plan your week in advance.** Ask yourself this question: what are the two or three main objectives that I must accomplish this week? Think in terms of those critical fires that must be put out, the ones that you would consider catastrophic if not completed by Friday. Tackle them quickly and effectively and move on.
2. **Schedule strategic time.** Dedicate at least ten percent of your week to strategic issues. This can include spending time developing the skills of your team, planning with colleagues and employees, conducting "system autopsies" of why your systems are not working, and spending time facilitating discussions on which processes can be improved and creating those systems. If you look at your week, break it down into ten segments: mornings and afternoons, five days a week. That gives you ten blocks of three and a half hours of time segments. Dedicate one of those segments to strategic issues. Start with Friday

afternoon when you probably spend most of your time thinking about the weekend anyway. Start with ten percent of your week and build from there. Time management is a myth. What is important is focus and execution. The areas that get attention generally improve over time and when you take a small sliver of your week and step back and look strategically at it, your effectiveness in managing your enterprise will improve.

3. **Make a list of all of the critical issues that you must accomplish for the week.** Ask yourself two questions: first, which ones can be delegated to someone else? And second, which ones can be used to develop a future leader in your department? Take what is on your plate and use it strategically as a development tool. You will find that next generation of leadership eager to assume more responsibility, so use your busy schedule as a way to identify and groom your future managers.

Think in terms of strategy whenever you do anything. When you start thinking this way, you will maximize your performance and start realizing your full potential as a manager. This simple concept can increase the effectiveness of a manager by at least thirty percent. Not only are you freeing up your day for more strategic issues, but you are using those tactical deadline oriented projects in a strategic manner. And if you follow those three steps to effective personal management, you'll never have to worry about anyone seeing that nervous little twitch again.

CHAPTER 7

MOSTLY GIVE

During the holidays at Annapolis, my classmates and I would do anything to get away from the rigors of a structured military environment for a few hours. So we sang Christmas carols at a nursing home out in town. It didn't really matter how good our singing was. Most of the residents were just happy to see someone other than a nurse holding a sharp pointy object, and we were just happy to see people who were happy to see us. One Sunday after we finished singing, we mingled with the elderly residents. I'll never forget meeting a young couple of lovebirds who had been married for over sixty years. I was mesmerized as I listened to their endearing story of how they first met, the tragedies that they faced, and how they had overcome them by keeping a strong faith and working very hard at their marriage. "You've obviously been very successful in your marriage," I said to my new friends. "What is the secret of your long and lasting relationship?"

The husband beamed back with a smile and said, "Give and take ... but mostly give."

I think his response is the secret of all lasting relationships, including those that we have at work. Give and take... but mostly give. What would it be like in your office if your entire team functioned with the attitude of "Mostly Give"? What would your customers think of you? How much repeat business would you have? How easy would it be for you to lead your employees with this attitude?

The concept of 'Mostly Give' is what builds organizations and helps them to stand the test of time, especially in the area of customer service. It's what makes the Early Girl Eatery in downtown Asheville my favorite restaurant for breakfast. If you ever want to see the concept of 'Mostly Give' in action, then eat your next breakfast there. First you get an authentic smile from the hostess, followed up with a quick and friendly visit from the waitress, topped off with good food and great service. And at the end of your meal, you know you'll be back, soon.

Living with the attitude of 'mostly give' is the fundamental premise of repeat business. We can't help ourselves when we are treated this way. We want more of it. We cannot have enough. We tire of poor service and self-centered sales people who fail to comprehend that the customer will never pay for anything that has no personal benefit to them. But if the sales rep figures out how to give more than what the customer will pay for, then they will have more business than they can handle. All relationships are give and take, but those that work and those that last are based on this premise.

This attitude of 'Mostly Give' applies to those in leadership roles as well. Think about the best boss you ever had. There was a reason why you were compelled to follow him or her, and that was probably based on this leadership concept. If we are following a leader who serves his team this way, then we will respond. We are wired, both through social conditioning and our psychological makeup, to respond in a cooperative and supportive manner to this type of leader. Striving to give more than you take is the best way to earn the trust of your employees. In fact, it is based on the principle of reciprocity as described in Robert Cialdini's book *Influence: Science and Practice*. If you extend a courtesy to someone else, then they are inclined to reciprocate that courtesy. If you are leading a team and extend trust, guidance, and encouragement, then they will reciprocate with trustworthiness, self-direction, and motivation.

The next time you engage someone else in a critical encounter, whether it's an employee, a colleague, or a customer, make an effort to exercise the attitude of 'mostly give' and see how positively and how long your relationship with them endures.

CHAPTER 8
IMPROVING TEAM ACCOUNTABILITY

"I'm so frustrated," he said to me. "I have a great strategic plan but I can't seem to get my people to follow it. I need you to help me develop an accountability system for my staff. I think we need more accountability."

My prospective consulting client was indeed frustrated. His 300-person organization was in a competitive industry at a time where many of his jobs were being shipped overseas, and he was pressured to do more with less and seemed to be getting more of less from his employees. The stress from shrinking margins, a shrinking pool of talent, and a shrinking client base all converged into a growing point of desperation.

"Bob," I said to him with a firm voice, "based on what you told me about your company, I don't think you have an accountability problem. I think you have an execution problem. Accountability is just the final step of teaching your people how to get things done. Once you build in a system of competent execution, creating an accountability system is just the icing on the cake. That's actually the fun part when you do it the right way."

If you face a problem similar to my client's, consider this five-step model to get your staff to start thinking more in terms of getting things done and less about you watching over their shoulder:

1. **The plan starts with the plan.** All of your staff, no matter where they sit on the food chain, needs to know about the direction of the company and the plan to take it there. If you hire an employee and fail to show him or her how they fit into the big picture, you are never going to see peak performance and maximum effort from that person. You might as well accept their contribution of being forty percent of what it could be.
2. **Make sure your team knows what is happening on the short-term horizon.** The long-term vision of the company is important, but most people don't even know what they're eating for lunch tomorrow. All they can think about is today. Keep the long term vision focused on the future, but the intense focus on the execution of what is required from them in the next thirty to ninety days. Remember, when we focus our intensity on a specific issue, and then the odds significantly increase that we'll get the results we're

looking for. Think of this communication, the act of telling them why their work matters, as the lens of the magnifying glass that is powerful enough to transform harmless sunrays into an energy that can ignite fire. *When we create a lens of focus, the intensity of our energy can give us explosive results*

3. **When you direct the efforts of your team, make sure you tell them why their work matters.** Tell them that their contribution on the project will help the department hit their target for the month and why that is important. Show them that the time they spend at work makes a difference in the lives of their colleagues. More than anything, we want to know our work makes a difference.
4. **Create an environment of open and honest feedback.** Let your team know that they can bring up information on what is not going right. This is something that must be witnessed by their own eyes for them to feel comfortable telling you that a problem exists somewhere in the process. If they witness anything to the contrary, you will never, ever, ever receive information you need to manage your organization effectively.
5. **Set up accountability systems that encourage peer accountability.** Create a 'buddy system' on the next project you are working on and measure the performance improvement. Let the team members choose which of their peers will keep them accountable for their specific issues. Test this model within your organization and see if it gets you better performance from your team. The ancillary benefits of this type

of system include (1) better teamwork, (2) improved cooperation among staff, (3) a chance to develop and observe prospective leaders within your organization, and (4) something different and fun. The thrill of group achievement bonds peers together into a cohesive unit. By giving them a chance to take control of their lives and help their colleagues, you increase the odds of execution with this type of amiable observation and accountability. Teach them to ask each other, "What's going to happen next and when?" When we start thinking in terms of execution, we get better at taking the actions we need to take. And when that happens, accountability doesn't really seem to be an issue anymore.

Remember that real leadership is invisible. At the end of the day you want the team to rise up and say, "We did this ourselves. This is our company, our team, our results." And when you achieve that level of integrating accountability into your plan of execution, work becomes meaningful, purposeful and fun.

CHAPTER 9
BECOMING "FOLLOWABLE"

I once gave a keynote address on leadership to a large group of mayors and city managers. Halfway through the program, I put them in groups of three or four and asked them all to come up with the five most important character qualities of a leader that they would follow anywhere.

One by one each group read out loud the first item on the list. "Someone who's honest." "A leader who can be trusted." "Tells the truth." "Follows their conscience." "Someone I know who won't speak with a forked tongue." "Integrity." This went on and on in different variations, but the point was clear. People want to follow those with some sort of a commitment to a belief system of ethics.

Contrast this with what you read about in the Wall Street Journal from time to time. CEO's proclaiming innocence and then getting found out through plea deals of former subordinate employees. There is indeed a crisis of leadership within our society.

On my first day as a midshipman at the Naval Academy, I learned what are known as the "Five Basic Responses." This is all you are allowed to say when an upperclassman addresses you during your first arduous year of structured adversity, known as "plebe year."

"Yes, sir/ma'am."
"No, sir."
"Aye aye, sir."
"I'll find out, sir." – used if they ask you something you don't know the answer to.
And the final one, "No excuse, sir."

This last response was given to an upperclassman when they asked why you didn't clean your room that day. You would like to tell them that you didn't have time because you spent all night studying your differential equations class because if you fail this exam, you'll get kicked out of the Academy. But you suck it up, and take the hit. "No excuse, sir!" you say, confidently accepting full responsibility for your inaction to clean your room.

This environment of radically brutal personal accountability teaches the future leaders of the fleet one of the critical lessons of leadership that most people would rather not learn: you are completely responsible for all that happens on your watch. You offer up no excuse, but take full responsibility for everything that happens while you are in charge. It's what your followers are craving. The only way you can lead and become worthy of having followers is to become "followable." By taking on the character qualities of leadership authenticity, you will have real followers who will seek to you for guidance, encouragement, leadership, and real substance worth following.

Take these three action steps in your own evaluation of your leadership skills:

1. **How do I see myself as a leader? Write in your journal a description of where you are currently in your leadership skills, and where you see yourself eventually growing.** Write as descriptively as possible.
2. **Ask yourself this question: What action steps do I need to take to become a leader worthy of followers?**
3. **Commit to a reading program of books on leadership.** Visit your local bookstore or Amazon and you'll see at least a hundred choices for you. Commit to reading only two pages a day.

Bonus tip: Have a weekly book review of books on leadership by your team. Read a chapter each week, and assign a verbal book report for each chapter by one of your teammates, rotating chapters among teammates. Go through a chapter each week and make it a fun exercise. Hold your discussion meetings during lunchtime on Fridays, and order pizza to make it fun.

By studying what leadership is and how you can implement it into your life, you will eventually become a leader whom anyone would consider "followable."

CHAPTER 10
FOLLOW YOUR MINESWEEPER

When I was a twenty-two year old Ensign in the early 1990's, I was third in command of a U.S. Navy minesweeper, which was built during the Korean War. Our ship was the oldest and the smallest ship in the fleet, quite insignificant and nearly invisible compared to carriers and cruisers. Yet when the Iraqis invaded Kuwait and we started training for combat operations, our level of importance increased because of the critical nature of our mission: to sweep live mines. When a small minesweeper leads larger ships through mine-infested harbors, she becomes the most important vessel in the fleet. At that point in time, the little boat makes a big difference because she can navigate their safe passage by allowing them to follow in her wake.

In your organization and in your career, find and follow your minesweeper. Quit trying to reinvent the wheel. Follow in the wake of those who already have sailed ahead of you successfully.

The easiest way to succeed in business is to replicate a model of proven success. Organizations win because of deliberate intention and effort, not random chance. There are four separate core competencies that a business organization must master to gain an edge: Leadership, Management, Execution, and Business Development.

Ask yourself this question: What causes my most successful competitors to succeed when others are not? Duplicate the proven model of success. You can adopt models of those four core competencies from leading competitors or similar organizations and apply what worked for them to your own model of success. Principles of success are malleable and transcend all industries.

Challenge yourself by following through this with these action items this week:

1. **On a sheet of paper, create a column for each of the four core competencies listed above.**
2. **Going over each core competency, ask yourself these questions and create a matrix, writing the answer in each column:**
   - "Where are my deficits in this area?"
   - "What do I need to do to achieve and overcome these deficits?"
   - "Right now, what are the biggest problems that I need to solve?"

3. **Write the name of someone who has succeeded in each of those areas.** You may know them personally or have heard of them.
4. **Politely ask them for a meeting and explain why you wish to meet with them.** Explore their model and consider duplicating it. Show them your list and ask for their advice. Ask them that if they were in your shoes, how would they solve those issues?
5. **Continue the relationship and follow up with them; all along you should ask them if there is anything you can do for them.** Don't just be a taker in this relationship; also be a giver.

What you are doing is cultivating a relationship with a mentor. Mentors are the key for success because they are giving you advice from the future. More than likely, they have already experienced the ups and downs that you experience. They can give you strategic guidance on how to navigate your way from the perspective of one who has already plotted the latitude and longitude of the mines that exist ahead of you. The danger zones are already marked on the chart. Use their chart and not yours and you'll avoid potentially catastrophic situations.

Some well-managed companies have formalized mentorship programs. When their junior managers join their company, they are assigned someone who is more experienced and already successful. This relationship benefits both parties, because in giving back to a mentee, you derive a personal benefit of knowing that you are contributing to the future success of a colleague and friend. It's truly a win/

win for the organization, the person you are mentoring, and you. Just knowing you can offer safe passage through dangerous waters to others can make all the difference in your own significance.

CHAPTER 11
POSITIVE INFLUENCE IN TIMES OF BAD NEWS

Question: How do I keep the morale of the organization high when I have to break bad news to them?

Answer: The morale of the team is the absolutely last thing a manager should consider when breaking bad news to employees. Focus on the health of the organization first. Morale will take care of itself.

Breaking bad news is a necessary part of being a manager. It's painful; it's difficult, and necessary to the normal high performance team. If you are with a company long enough, it is something that cannot be avoided. And just like being in a healthy marriage or relationship, it is possible to share in the experience of going through a difficult experience together, and end up with a stronger relationship.

Although morale is important, it ranks below other factors on the hierarchy of needs of an organization, such as mission accomplishment, team unity, and group effectiveness. Morale is usually a byproduct of a healthy organization, and never should be the focus of a manager. Morale grows on its own out of a high performance team when a manager has the right intentions of developing the team in the proper way, with the right amount of balanced focus on mission accomplishment.

The effective leader does not have to worry about the morale levels when bringing bad news to a group. Instead, he should keep the health of the organization intact and a top priority. The health of the organization is determined by:

1. The effectiveness of the group.
2. Team unity, measured at the lowest level of the food chain.
3. Team ownership of the mission.
4. Employees' emotional intelligence (their knowledge and understanding of how their emotions impact them at work, and how to manage those emotions productively).
5. The team's commitment to be involved in the development of leaders at every level.

If these elements of a group are intact, then the manager has a healthy organization. And if he does, then when he gives bad news to a group, then the group will learn how to deal with that bad news themselves.

With this right perspective of leadership, the manager can feel confident that his or her team will be able to take the bad news, process it in a healthy manner, and deal with the change with an increased level of team unity and team effectiveness.

CHAPTER 12
SHOW HOW THEIR WORK MATTERS

I met with a prospective client for the very first time, a very large international manufacturing company. The receptionist warmly greeted me by introducing herself, welcoming me to her company, and extending her hand professionally. That's the first time in my entire life that a receptionist shook hands with me, and I loved it. In a single moment, I learned four things about this multi-national corporation:

1. This receptionist took ownership of her space by welcoming me to it. This demonstrated personal accountability and pride in the workplace.
2. She understood her role as both the 'director of first impressions' and the 'final memory-maker' of the company. That means that she either came up with this protocol on her own or someone trained her on it. If she herself developed this protocol of

greeting visitors, then that means that the manager who hired her figured out how important it is to put people who take initiative in this highly visible role. They choose not to settle when they hired her.
3. Or, if she was trained on this protocol, then that means this is a company that places a priority on training. If they train the receptionist on how to greet visitors, then they probably have strong training in place in larger functions. If you excel in the little things, then you'll excel in the major areas.
4. Someone up the food chain probably told her why her job matters, and that matters significantly. She knows that her job is important and helps the company reach its objectives.

People need to know that their work matters. Think about it. We spend more time with our co-workers than we do our loved ones, and employees need to know the direct contribution that is made to the company through their work. Can you imagine spending your entire career doing something that makes no difference? More than anything, people want to be fulfilled. I have personally engaged tens of thousands of executives in conversations about leadership, loyalty, and career issues. One of the biggest motivators of employees is for them to know that what they do all day counts for something.

Next time you hire a new employee, tell him or her not just what your expectations are, but how their work impacts the organization. Be specific. Show the big picture. Draw out the organizational chart for his department and show

how his contribution affects the team, and how the team affects the company's direction. Do you want your employees to perform with their heart and soul? Then you need to reach them in the area of the heart and soul so that in times of a crunch, they can put forth the extra efforts that are required. In the case of my new client, the receptionist was creating a strong positive image of the company with a prospective business partner.

Here are three action steps for you to take. Try them and see how motivated your employees become:

1. **During your next performance review, be specific about the contribution your employee made in the overall direction of the company.** Even if it's a clerk or an intern, show why his job matters.
2. **Ask if there is anything you can do to help your employee do his job better.** People really want to make a contribution, but first they must know what that contribution is. Once they know, then they are open to seeing their role in different ways and will be open to your leadership in helping them perform better.
3. **Ask yourself the following question: What are the ways that I can serve my staff and help them perform better?** Journal about this question in the next two days. See what sort of ideas you come up with.

Remember that each employee counts and makes a difference. And when they know this specifically, you will see a marked difference in their performance.

CHAPTER 13
CATALYST MANAGEMENT

As a liberal arts major and a non-scientific thinker, I nearly failed Chemistry at Annapolis in the first semester of my junior year. But during the second semester, I was put in the "special" Chemistry class for the scientifically challenged. It was just the football team and me. I felt right at home.

I don't remember much of the curriculum of that class but I did learn what a catalyst was. A catalyst is a type of compound or chemical that when added to other chemicals initiates a measurable change in the properties of those chemicals, resulting in a reaction with a visible color change, smell, or even an explosion. Without this catalyst, the compounds and energy attributes of the chemicals remain dormant and unchanging.

As a manager, your job is to manage the chemistry of your team, specifically the four types of energy that your employees bring to work with them every day. Each person brings mental energy, emotional energy, physical energy, and commitment energy into your workplace. This is the energy capital that you have to manage. It is your job to manage the flow of these four attributes and work with them in a way that solves your problems. Or better yet, develop a culture that causes your team to intentionally and willingly manage their own energy in the accomplishment of the desired objectives.

In some organizations, employees do the minimum just to get by. If minimum wasn't good enough, it wouldn't be minimum, they say to themselves. But it is this fourth energy, the commitment energy, which is the catalyst for the other three. Separate the other three and focus on the fourth. If you learn how to foster the growth of this commitment energy, you will see a chain reaction and combustion of excitement and enthusiasm within your organization in the emotional, mental, and physical energy areas of your staff.

Here are three ways to incite this growth of commitment energy:

1. **Become the type of leader who is followable.** There is no such thing as professional leadership. There is only personal leadership. Leadership is intensely personal and it all starts with you. Success in this area does not rely on chance, but instead is deliberate. Start by reading two pages a day from a leadership book. Begin with *Intrinsic Motivation at Work*

by Dr. Kenneth Thomas, which explains this energy model in greater detail. It is an easy and pithy read, full of solid nuts and bolts about leadership that offers insight and potent take-home value.

2. **Ask questions.** Ask questions of your staff and listen. Listen with empathy and repeat their answers back to them to make sure you understood what they said.
3. **Set up accountabilities between co-workers.** Instead of holding an employee accountable for all of his tasks, delegate some of those accountabilities to one of his peers. This not only clears your mind from just one more thing to think about, but also develops leadership among your employees in its purest form: peer leadership. Peer leadership thrives on legitimate influence and the careful balance of political capital because of the nature of how we want to be seen and treated by our colleagues. If you're a bad peer leader then no one will invite you to the party. This system of peer accountability is not just more effective, but also keeps you from having to act like a boss all the time. Plus, it's more fun for your employees when they take an interest in trying to solve each others' problems instead of hearing you rant and rave once again about their performance.

By fanning the flames on the fire of commitment energy in your team, you will achieve explosive results, better morale, and tighter relationships among peers. And you get to use this catalyst without ever having to open a Chemistry textbook again.

CHAPTER 14
CHANGING THE CULTURE OF A COMPANY

The culture of a company is the significant driving force that resists being measured but can always be felt. It is that set of beliefs, premises, and emotions which are living and experienced by all members of the team. Everyone knows the culture that exists within his own company. You can feel it from the very first day that you show up for work. But if your company's culture is counter to its effectiveness, how do you go about changing it?

Some organizations experience a culture that is incongruent with achieving its goals, or might even be opposed to the very existence and mission of that organization. Many well-intentioned managers try to change their company's culture in a way that is ineffective and even detrimental to the life of the team. They misunderstand that culture is an organic development and not a mandate. Although it can be influenced by outside forces and senior management, it will never be held captive to the desires of a tight-fisted captain.

It is the shaping and harnessing of this culture that has been the Holy Grail of many managers. This is what I call the "culture trap", when managers try to shape the culture with ineffective means and end up creating a force that is more damaging than what they had to begin with. They try to steer the culture into a direction of raising the bar, but instead exacerbate their very problem by influencing it in the direction of micromanagement, fear, and distrust. I have even seen CEO's embark on a voyage of pretentious futility by creating a position similar to a "culture czar" or "minister of culture." Culture can never be institutionalized. To even try is folly.

Instead of forcing a culture change on a company, you must simply allow that change to happen. You cannot change the direction of a river. But you can channel it through a dam and harness its energy to provide power for an entire city. Don't think in terms of changing and dictating the type of culture you would like to see evolve in your group. Instead, channel and direct the efforts of your organization by leading with authenticity.

Follow these three steps to positively influencing and shaping the culture of your company:

1. **Spend time in the field.** Get to know the people who make up your organization. Carve out at least ten

percent of your time every other week to mix and mingle with the line workers on the plant floor and listen to them tell you about their challenges. You might not have the solution, but at least you took time to listen. Listening to your employees helps you build good will and shows that your intentions are authentic. In the world of leadership development and culture change, sometimes the intentions are good enough.
2. **Understand the grievances and complaints and issues that all of your staff bring to you.** Sometimes you might disagree with the person who is bringing you the complaint, and it's fine to tell them of your difference so long as you first hear them out and let them know that they have been understood. There is a crisis of understanding in our society. Understand the issues of your people and empathize with them.
3. **Live in a way that is congruent with the values of your company.** If respect is a core value of your organization and you blew off the meeting you scheduled with a prospective vendor, then you are lacking in your authenticity and it will be felt in other areas of the organization. Every interaction with those who work in your company and those who come in contact with it will shape the way your culture develops within your organization. As a leader, you are always on display.

Lead your team with authenticity and congruence, and watch your culture rise to a level that contributes to your team's effectiveness.

CHAPTER 15

THE CHRONIC COMPLAINER

The frequent complainer should be transferred to the basement, the satellite office in Alaska, or terminated.

Those who complain and do not display a positive attitude are contributing to the demise of the team. They are a negative cancer that spreads unless it is either treated with radioactive-level consulting and counseling, or amputated to save the rest of the body. It is a critical issue of management that a manager keeps the morale of his or her department at a peak level in order to have a peak performance level, and any manager who tolerates someone like this is either inexperienced, incompetent, or inherited the company.

If someone does have a reason to complain, but does it with the right degree of delicacy, then I would recommend listening to that person with a wary ear but an open mind. Perhaps their dissension does warrant attention.

Probably the most shocking statement from a CEO that I've ever heard them say to a subordinate who was straying away from the party line was, "Now that's not a very career-enhancing statement." No, but it was probably just what the group needed to hear because the emperor wasn't wearing any clothes; but if you point this out, you need to do so with a very high degree of tact and delicacy, and chances are, if your complaining colleague has a point, you should delve into it further. Make sure you can separate the fact from the feeling, though, when you do this. Disregard hearsay and pay attention only to the facts of an issue and the perspective of that experienced employee. And if this employee who might appear a bit cranky is professionally adept at their skill areas, then heed what they say, but tell them to tone down the negativity.

There are three steps to dealing with the complainer if they happen to be a colleague of yours:

1. **Listen with an open mind.** Perhaps they are complaining, or perhaps they are right. Tune out their emotionalism and negative attitude. Pay attention to the words they are saying and test for their validity.
2. **Take action on what they say.** If they have a point, take action on it and see if it makes sense. If they turn out to be clueless, then disregard everything else that they ever tell you. If they're just complaining to make noise and they don't work for you, then you can't terminate them. You can counsel them, though, on the merits of having a positive mental

attitude, but in my experience people never change unless there is a life-enhancing reason to change.
3. **If you have the authority, consider hiring a consultant.** If their attitude needs a boost, hire the expertise of a consultant that specializes in that area. Check references on previous work experience to make sure that you get your money's worth.

By helping those individuals in your group who really wish to change, you not only keep the team unity intact, but the whole team will be grateful for your initiative to solve a very vocal and visible problem.

CHAPTER 16
CLARIFY EXPECTATIONS WITH NEW EMPLOYEES

He was upset and it showed. I could hear it in his voice. "Scott, when I told him I was not happy with his work performance and that I was terminating him, he just stared at me and his face turned white. He actually thought he was performing well in his role as one of our key executives." My client went on to tell me that their final meeting lasted over two and a half hours, and concluded in a mutual explosion of emotion. The fired employee ran out yelling vulgar profanities, full of feelings of hostility and disbelief. My client, a dignified CEO of a large professional services firm, just sat there in solitude after the meeting with feelings of emptiness and hollowness. And then he wondered if he made the right decision in terminating his employee.

"Tell me about the direction and expectations you gave the employee when you first hired him last April," I said.

"What are you talking about?" he responded. "I just hired him and expected him to do what he was supposed to do. He's been in this industry a long time. He should know what his job is."

"So, what you're telling me is that through your mental telepathy and his psychic abilities, you were thinking that he could read your mind to know what was expected of him without you clearly expressing it… is that what you're saying?" Actually, I didn't say this. That's the message I gave him though in my 'tough love' style.

"I see your point," he said. My client discovered for the very first time that he never clearly communicated his expectations of performance to the new hire, and that the employee honestly thought he was performing well in his role.

When you bring on a new employee, how do you clarify the performance expectations to increase the odds of a productive and happy work relationship between you and your new hire? Follow these three steps the next time you bring on a new member of your team. These are ideas I learned from Lou Adler:

1. **Tell your new hire what the expectations are.** Move beyond duties and responsibilities and enter into the realm of very clear and specific expectations. Use these SMART objectives: How do you **Specifically** define success? How do you **Measure** success? What **Action** steps need to be taken for them to be

considered successful? What are the **Results** you need? What **Timelines** are associated with these issues?
2. **Ask them how they see themselves performing at their peak performance levels in that role.** What is their action plan to achieve their goals? How will they use their past experiences to hit their targets? What specific steps need to be taken?
3. **Set up an ongoing system to measure their progress toward goal achievement.** But even before you and your new hire establish goals, you need to make sure that this new employee knows how the role fits in exactly with the accomplishment of the team goals. Show the big picture. Draw out an organizational chart so they can see where they fit in relation to everyone else. Show them exactly how their individual contribution helps the team reach its level of collective achievement. Show them why they matter to you and to their colleagues on a personal level. Leadership is very personal, so you need to bring those expectations to the personal level.

Hopefully, by beginning the relationship with proper expectations, you will help your staff perform at their peak performance levels, which means that both you and your team will be pleased with how the working relationship develops. And you'll never find yourself in the position of terminating an employee who thought they were succeeding.

CHAPTER 17
CLARIFYING CORE VALUES

In 1994, Jim Collins and Jerry Porras wrote a book called *Built to Last*. The book is a comparative analysis between companies that compete in the same markets and have similar beginnings, and shows why some are wildly successful and the others are not. The premise is this: companies which focus on clarifying and articulating set of core values and focusing on a distinct mission are able to outpace their competitors and will end up far ahead of the rest.

This leadership model became a fast-growing issue in the field of organizational development. So the race was on. Companies flocked to corporate retreat centers to develop their own sets of core values. This concept of value initiatives has become a hallmark of well-intentioned organizations that try to duplicate the patterns of success in legendary corporations, and for the most part it works.

But here's the danger when a company sets out to implement this model. When you clarify your core values as an organization you are saying, "These are our beliefs and we will never deviate from these values. They are at the top of our hierarchy of actions. Everything we do will be congruent with these values." Few companies are willing to make this sort of statement because of our own mortal need for self-preservation. But this important concept of committing to the core set of your guiding premises is what Abraham Maslow called self-actualization in his hierarchy of needs. It is the same reason why our grandfathers invaded Normandy against a phalanx of bullets and the same reason why Rosa Parks didn't give up her bus seat.

When we believe in a set of core values so much that we are willing to risk our own self-preservation to achieve them, then we are congruent in our actions and are free to perform at our peak levels. It's a tall order for most organizations but the potential to live this way exists within each one of us.

There are three pitfalls that a company must avoid in identifying and clarifying core values.

1. **You could be setting yourself up for failure as an organization.** In fact, if you and your management team clarify your core values and make them part of your culture, then you risk losing credibility and trust among your employees if you are not congruent in following them. For example, if an employee sees

a senior level executive ridiculing a direct report in a meeting, and one of the core values of the company is respect, then the leadership team loses trust with that employee and all the others who hear about the incident. And remember that bad news travels faster than good news.
2. **When organizations set out to develop their core values and miss the mark, their intention is not so much misguided as misunderstood.** They might list values that they would like to have but are not the driving force of their premises, values that are more aspirational than core. The core values are those premises that govern all aspects of the company.
3. **This is not an initiative that can be delegated to human resources with no further thought from the top.** This issue is so critical that it must become a core competency of the CEO and his or her direct reports. The clarification of core values should not be an event used to simply generate a temporary buzz of excitement from a one-day retreat. "Hey, look at us. We clarified our core values. Now get back to work." Instead, it must come from the founder, the leadership team, the employees with a significant stake and tenure in the company, and the real contributors. It is more a process of discovery than a single discussion.

Initiate a dialogue with your colleagues about the driving premises that govern your company's behavior, and watch how the congruence of that behavior swells in the hearts, the minds, and the performance of your team.

CHAPTER 18
CLEANING UP SOMEONE ELSE'S MESS

I was in a Starbucks picking up a quick cup of coffee. As I walked over to the counter to mix in my half-in-half, I noticed that a puddle of milk sat at the counter that was spilled by a previous customer.

Not my spill, I thought to myself. So I ignored it and continued stirring my coffee. Clean me up, it said to me. No way. You are not my problem. I looked at it. It looked back. We just sort of had this staring contest, me and the puddle of milk that had probably been sitting there for at least an hour.

Okay, I can't stand it anymore. I'll wipe it up. Even though it wasn't my responsibility, even though I really didn't care that much about it, even though no one was paying me to clean it up, there was something about abandoning the wet counter that didn't feel right. For some reason it almost went against my nature. As I was wiping it up I realized why I felt that way. "Always leave the camp site better than when you found it," my scoutmaster told me when I was a youth. It was in the Boy Scouts that I first learned this concept of stewardship.

This leadership lesson of stewardship, wanting to make things better than when you found them, is irresistible to both employees and customers. It helps build team unity, attract customers to you, gets your staff working together to help each other out, and makes you a better manager. Here are three ways to integrate this way of thinking into your business model:

1) **Foster the attitude of responsibility.** When you work on a project, even though someone else started it, you own it. If you are involved in any way, then you have a responsibility to make it better. If you started working for a company and the division is a mess from the manager before you, then you need to clean it up. You own it. And every time you complain about your predecessor to your staff and your colleagues, your own direct reports are thinking that it's okay to ignore spills caused by other employees. By not fostering and encouraging the attitude of stewardship, you are fostering and encouraging the attitude of 'it's not my problem.'
2) **Get over it and focus on the solution.** Forget about who was at the counter before you and spilled the creamer. It doesn't really matter. So what if the

department's previous manager didn't keep the staff accountable. Maybe the numbers weren't hit last year. That was last year and there's nothing you can do about it. Anytime you shift the blame and focus on something other than the solution, it weakens your brand in the market. If you are a manager, then your employees are your customers. By taking full ownership of the results, you attract them to you. In our own human nature, we cannot help but be attracted to those who follow these principles of leadership.

3) **Take this concept and develop the attitude within your team.** Jack Welch believed in cross training; it was one of his hallmarks as a leader at GE. To effectively cross-train and get your staff positively involved in each other's business, stewardship needs to be assimilated into your culture. When everyone wants to make the entire campsite better than when they found it, then it's easy to develop the processes to cross-train managers and staff.

When your staff sees you pitching in and contributing to departments other than yours, they will be more inclined to serve each other. When we start thinking about what benefits all of us, the group as a whole, then it's easier to develop the positive feelings of actually wanting to help each other. And that always makes for a better campsite.

CHAPTER 19
CONFLICT RESOLUTION: A NEW APPROACH

Most employee work agreements and other legal documents start with something like this: "I think that eventually you might try to damage me in some way, so I'm creating this document and requiring you to sign it to protect me."

Start your next important business relationship with a different type of document, the State of Grace Document. This is an agreement that commits to resolving all future differences in an agreeable fashion, in terms of a mutual satisfaction of needs. Relationships take work, especially those that you have at work. And in all relationships conflict is inevitable. Instead of separating the two parties into warring factions, this document brings them together to seek a positive resolution.

According to the management consultants who are the originators of this agreement, Maureen McCarthy and Zelle Nelson in Flat Rock, NC, this concept has improved operational performance, employee loyalty, and conflict resolution skills of organizations all over the world.

There are five parts to the State of Grace Document:

1. **"The Story of Us". Share your story of what attracted you to each other.** Why did you join your company? What was it that you saw in this prospective employee that caused you to hire him or her? What were your motives at the initial phase of your relationship? At this point you are documenting those things that caused you to want to join the company or the reasons why you hired that key employee. You are gaining clarification on why the relationship decided to start in the first place. Specifically, write out those tangible items that you saw in the other party that caused you to want to establish the relationship and the feelings that you felt at the beginning.
2. **Work Styles and Warning Signs.** Each of you will have a chance to voice your preferences at work. Do you want the door open or closed? What are your preferences of how you want to be managed? What sort of communication do you expect from your staff? And what are those warning signs, the symptoms, of how you show that you are under stress? "Check in with me when you see me start to…" For example, "When I start to isolate, please initiate conversation with me. At that point, I need your help

more than ever, even when I tell you that everything is fine." This gives us permission to approach and initiate communication when we sense that things are starting to move out of the balance of harmony.
3. **Expectations.** What are the expectations of performance that you need from your staff? What are the expectations that they need from you? What are the core values and premises that guide this relationship?
4. **List of Questions.** If we get in a bad place, what are the things that a third party mediator should ask us to bring us on track? "Are things going as planned?" "Have I let you down in some way?" Not only should you establish a procedure of questions to bring focus back to a harmonious state, but you should limit or clarify a time frame that you commit to each other to resolve these questions, such as three hours. Within three hours, each of you could commit to checking in with each other to ask these questions when you start to see the warning signs listed in step two.
5. **Long Term Agreement.** Leave the door open over the long term. This gives permission to either party to bring resolution of past conflicts that may take time from which to heal. And even if the conflict is so bad that you cannot find resolution, at least you agree to return to a state of grace over the long term.

By beginning your next business relationship this way, you are not setting up protective measures for conflict but systems that allow for resolution of conflict, which is always inevitable.

CHAPTER 20
LEADERSHIP DEVELOPMENT ON A BUDGET

"How important is it to you to develop your managers?" I asked my prospective client. He was a second-generation owner of a large distribution company and had been running the family business for just a few years.

"What do you mean?" he asked.

"On a scale of one to ten, ten meaning it's most important, how important is it for your managers to effectively lead their teams?"

"Well, a ten I suppose," he responded.

"So what specific steps have you taken to develop your managers' abilities to lead their people effectively?" I asked again. He mumbled something about it not being his area of responsibility and I sort of responded that if he didn't want the responsibility of developing his managers then his best competitors would be happy to assume it. The conversation quickly waned to a weak conclusion and I knew that my advice was falling on deaf ears.

Remember that all of your employees are temporary employees, and if you fail to develop them as leaders then there are many companies with bigger budgets and better training opportunities that are willing to do so. Each day you must prove your worth as a leader to your employees, and by developing their skill sets in their abilities to lead their people then you are giving them one more reason to stay with you and one more reason to try harder for you.

"What happens if I develop my staff and they leave?" one client asked me.

"What happens if you don't develop them and they stay?" I responded.

Leadership development is a critical priority for every business owner and senior level executive in an organization. If you have a limited budget in this area, then consider the following three ideas that you can implement right away.

1. **Develop an informal study of leadership within your company.** Leadership is a concept that must be continuously studied. If you have a limited budget than you can do what Jim Nargane started with his company, Ryan Construction, a large developer and

general contractor in Minneapolis. He kicked off a book club where each week his team of managers would read one chapter from a leadership book and discuss it on Fridays during lunch. He would rotate the group facilitator each week and give all of them a chance to lead the chapter review and facilitate a dialogue on the issues learned from the book. Just by talking about this critical topic you can infuse a leadership culture into the organization and spark energy and interest in the subject.

2. **Take that dialogue of leadership and seek feedback from your managers on how they witness it in action at work.** Bob Roberts, a banking executive in Asheville, NC, holds a monthly meeting with his managers. The first item on the agenda is to listen to stories of leadership in action. They get these stories straight from the trenches, from what they witness first-hand in their individual branches. By developing an open and frank discussion on the issues in the field, they are raising the leadership consciousness.

3. **Roberts also meets with each manager once a quarter to discuss their own personal leadership development.** He asks them to list their top three personal behavior goals, and asks his managers to grade themselves in each of those categories. Roberts says that he puts it in terms of this question: "What can we do to help you get better at _____?" By phrasing the question this way, he is relying on legitimate influence from the standpoint of authentic leadership to develop his staff and less on his position of authority. People respond to those leaders who give them

room to develop their own ideas, even those ideas that have to do with personal leadership. When a subordinate manager tells you how he will solve his own problems, then you have just instilled a sense of ownership and taken one more item off of your to-do list at the same time.

Leadership development doesn't have to be expensive. It just has to be done. Consider making it a priority in your organization today and see the difference it makes in the performance of your team.

CHAPTER 21
FOCUS ON THE PERSONAL BENEFIT

The frustrated sales rep became annoyed with me when I told her that I really didn't see any reason to buy her product. She tried close number 17 on me, right after rebuttal number 34. "Would you like for me to just give you some money?" I asked her. She seemed puzzled and asked me what I meant. "I am getting the feeling that all you want is your commission. I feel like you don't care about how your product can benefit me personally because you haven't shown me that. I feel like all you really want is your commission and that your heart isn't committed to benefiting me through your product."

She left my office frustrated and confused because she didn't get the sale. I went back to work puzzled why a sales manager would spend so much time training a sales rep on the tactics of the sale but neglect the key component to effective sales relationships: knowledge of the personal benefits of the product or service, and how to effectively communicate those personal benefits.

Forget about sales tactics. Instead, focus on buying motives. I first learned this concept from my friend Jeffrey Gitomer, a successful sales trainer in Charlotte, NC. If you are selling your product or service to your customer and you have nothing else in mind but to serve your prospect, then it will come through to them and make the sale much easier to close.

People hate to have the feeling that they are being sold something. But the typical sales professional keeps using sales trick number 19 that was first developed in 1972, hoping to close their prospect without any regard for the potential benefit to the end user. What worked in the past in the profession of selling won't work today.

Consider this concept. Forget about features and benefits. Nobody really cares about the features and benefits of your products and services. Instead, they care about their own personal benefits that are derived from your product or service. People only make decisions that personally benefit them, so that's what you need to target with your prospect. If you are in sales, you can develop authentic and meaningful relationships with your prospects when you think this way.

Here are three ways to develop a solid sales plan based on the buying motives of those you wish to reach:

1. **Consider your own product or service.** Find out why the past ten customers bought from you. The reasons you think they purchased it might be totally different from their real reasons, so you need to find out what they are. Call them and ask them to tell you the three issues that made them buy from you before the product was delivered, and looking back, why they would buy it all over again.
2. **Ask your prospect why he or she would buy it, before you even go in to your presentation.** Ask this question before you even present your product or service: "What criteria is important to you in the purchase of a widget?" Find out EXACTLY what is important to them, simply by asking them. Congratulations, champ. You now have a buying motive. Sell to that motive, not to what you think it might be.
3. **With your colleagues, determine what the personal benefits of your product or service are by drilling down with these questions:** First, what are the features of my product? Second, what are the benefits? Third, what are the benefits of those benefits? And fourth, how would a prospect benefit from this product or service on the personal level? Why would they benefit from this product on a personal level? What would those personal benefits be? When would they be realized?

Minor changes in major areas are the essence of real and lasting achievement. Make these minor modifications in your selling skills and watch your revenue increase.

CHAPTER 22
THE FOUR M'S OF PERFORMANCE IMPROVEMENT

One of my speaking clients, an executive with a large and well-managed bank, asked me to consider consulting with them on performance improvement. He knew that the time to work on getting to the next level isn't when you are in a crisis, but when things are relatively stable and productive. When I asked him about potential places for performance improvement, he responded with some specific areas in which he felt that assistance from someone on the outside would offer a fresh and challenging perspective.

When he asked me how I would go about solving some of their issues, I told him, "We don't know exactly what the real issues are in your company at this point. You might think that the noise from your car's engine means that the timing belt will soon need to be replaced, but if we investigate it further we might find that it's only the loose change rattling in your ash tray. Let's first investigate and pinpoint some root issues facing you right now, then we'll come up with a plan of action for resolution and improvement."

In order to find those potential improvement areas within your organization, even when things are going well, consider this simple model what I call the Four M'S of Performance Improvement:

1. **Metrics.** Anything that can be measured generally improves over a period of time. I first learned this when I was a twenty-four year old internal organizational development consultant in the Navy. It was in the early nineties that the Navy rolled out a leadership initiative using W. Edwards Deming's management methods, otherwise known as Total Quality Management. Deming's message of continuous improvement also included a component of knowing what improvements need to be continuously made and in what areas. And when you eagerly start making improvements, you need to make sure that you're not chasing the wrong areas to improve. Did that change you make recently really improve the bottom line? How do you know? If it's measurable, it's real.
2. **Motivation.** The gas in the car is what makes it go. Your staff needs to operate from a place of intrinsic motivation. It's not the incentive package that you worked so hard to create that will keep them keeping on. It's not the trip at the end of the year. It's not the browbeating and the heat they feel from the boss.

It's the burn within the belly that compels them to do what they should do, even when they don't feel like it. And when people can consciously choose to perform at their peak levels even when they don't want to, they will run circles around the competition. The internal motivation of your team is what will give your company an edge, and remember that an edge, no matter how small, is still an edge. And sometimes that's all you need to win the race.

3. **Message.** What is the message that is brought to the market about your company? How specific is it? Do you sell your customers on the fact that you are the oldest manufacturing company in your niche or the fact that you can solve their personal problems when they buy your product? Your message will miss the mark if you don't bring clarity in showing your customers why they benefit personally from doing business with organization. It doesn't matter how slick your new website is if it doesn't say anything about how your customers benefit on a personal level from doing business with you.

4. **Meaning.** Why do your people come to work every day? If I asked you what the vision of your company is, would you respond that it's to put money in the shareholders' pockets? If that is the case, then do you really think your staff will go to the wall when they need to? It's your job as a leader to crystallize the long term and emotional vision of what your organization or even your department will look like in the future, and start talking about it.

The time to make serious headway in performance improvement isn't when things are going wrong. It's when they're going well. Use this model to analyze your business and make a commitment today to work it to the next level. When you do, you will grow in your influence and authenticity as you build relationships that directly impact performance.

CHAPTER 23
GIVING CONTROL TO THE TEAM

I don't think there's a single employee in the world of work who likes to be micro-managed. But I can't say I don't blame managers for wanting to try to control everything with their staff. Their careers are on the line and the targets have to be met each month. The manager is responsible for all results and outcomes of the team. If it's an owner who's managing the operation of his own company, then even his personal credit rating is at stake with each purchase of product and inventory. The pressure can be intense for managers to achieve results and many times there appears to be no other option except to manage with a command and control mindset.

But if these well-intentioned company managers don't find better methods to reach the targets of their group then they will burn out and burn bridges. They'll run out of the time and energy required to stay sharp and they'll run out of people who will end up sticking around to be pushed around.

The role of a leader is to create an environment that incites and inspires the team to want to perform. Your team should take ownership to develop solutions themselves and willingly implement them. In fact, true leadership is invisible. At the end of the day, you want the team to say, "We did this ourselves. This was our problem, and we found the solution. We own it and we solved it all by ourselves."

Consider opening up this discussion when you meet at your next staff meeting:

1. **Tell your employees what you perceive to be the ideal outcome.** Ask for their input and agreement on this outcome.
2. **Ask them what action steps they need to take to achieve the outcome.** If you tell them what to do then you are still a boss. If they come up with the ideas themselves then you are now a leader. When they come up with the idea, then it's theirs and they own it. And if they own it, then they're committed to doing it. And if they're committed, then the odds increase that things will actually get done.
3. **Steer them away from potential catastrophes, but give them latitude to make mistakes. And when they do, use mistakes as learning moments.** I've heard of some executives that gives small bonuses to employees each time they make a mistake. Once the mistake happens, quietly pull the employee aside

and discuss the issue. Ask questions such as, "What would you do over again if you had the chance?" I have even created tools for sales teams called "Deal Autopsies" where they can pick through deals that fell apart so they can use the carcass of the dead deal as a teaching tool.
4. **Ask your employees about target dates.** What do they believe is a realistic target date for the final outcome?
5. **Ask "Would it be okay if I kept you accountable at these benchmark dates?"** Most people won't have a problem being asked. As a manager you have the right to check on anything they are doing at any time anyway. But when you ask for permission you are earning a follower and gaining buy-in for completion.
6. **Follow up with this question with your employee: "Is there anything that I can do to help you reach this outcome?"** This will open doors to solutions and will build a better working relationship.

Remember, more than anything, we all want to be in control of our lives. And if you follow these steps you'll never hear anyone complaining about not having the chance to do it themselves.

CHAPTER 24

HIRING YOUR CUSTOMER

A few years back on a consulting assignment, I was helping a large privately owned company to develop a strategy for attracting new employees. They wanted to be the employer of choice in their industry, and were in an aggressive growth phase. The executive vice president was a very likable fellow and came across as an "Andy Griffith" type, someone who was everybody's best friend. He had a very impressive demeanor, could persuade prospective employees very easily, and could sell the company. He was one of the best I've ever seen at having the natural and intuitive ability of attracting new talent. But he had the absolute worst track record of hiring them. It doesn't matter how many fish bite the line if you can't land them in the boat.

His schedule was intense. He traveled all the time, worked weekends, and always had at least six or seven irons in the fire. His assistant almost needed another assistant to keep up with his workload. He took on a large part of the company's growth, while simultaneously managing a $100 million a year branch office. And he was responsible for hiring all key staff throughout most offices of the company.

Because he was so busy fighting fires, he naturally prioritized. The fires quickest to reach his feet received his attention, and everything else was on the back burner. The only problem with his strategy was that all good candidates were ignored and they eventually lost interest. The hiring scenarios were so far removed from his immediate attention because those fires were far away in the future and could be dealt with "later"…whenever that is. By not keeping up with the rhythm of his searches and interviews, the good candidates assumed that he was a poor manager and assumed falsely that he was absent-minded, scattered, and unfocused. After receiving a candidate's resume, an initial telephone call would be scheduled, which he would consistently forget about, leaving the candidate wondering why the call never came. The calls were rescheduled, and if he didn't forget about them, he kept pushing them back. It would take him as long as four weeks to connect with an interested candidate. And finally, when he had the time to interview, the candidate would withdraw his candidacy and move on to another opportunity, carrying a bad taste of that company in their mouth forever.

The problem of making hiring a priority affects every organization. We cannot help but attack those issues that affect us the soonest, which leaves hiring relegated to another time. Remember that hiring directly affects cash flow and long-term survivability more than any other issue. Here's a solution for the teachable executive who can see the value of hiring top talent: make that prospective employee your customer. Yes, your customer. Treat them as if they bring several hundred thousands of dollars of net income to your company every year... because they do. If you can realize and understand the quantifiable impact that a star employee has on your company, you would rarely neglect them.

Call them when you say you're going to call them. Write them thank-you notes or send a nice email to them. Yes, you the employer should write a star prospect a short note telling them how glad you were to meet them. Take them out to lunch. Wine them and dine them. But most importantly, keep the hiring process on the front burner, even when more urgent issues may seem critical. If you neglect to keep this hiring process a priority, you eventually will not have to worry about it.

CHAPTER 25
TAKE ADVANTAGE OF YOUR ADVANTAGE

I was flying to a speaking engagement and was changing planes in the Charlotte airport, walking to the gate for my next flight in terminal E. I was ahead of schedule but still maintained my normal brisk airport pace, something of a mix between a fast walk and a slow run. I eased my way onto the 'moving sidewalk' and saw that half the people ahead of me on the machine were just standing there, letting the sidewalk move them forward at a snail's pace.

"What's wrong with you people?" I wanted to scream. "You have an advantage, now use it! Just because the sidewalk moves you along doesn't give you an excuse to be lazy! Get moving!" I looked to the right of the moving sidewalk and saw that those people who were walking at their normal pace on the normal floor of the terminal were passing the stationary passengers riding the moving sidewalk. How sad,

I thought to myself. Here they are on a machine designed to accelerate their forward movement and move them quicker to their end destination and they are choosing not to use it. Instead, those without the advantage are passing them.

In the world of business, the advantage that you have over your competitor doesn't guarantee your success. In fact, it could be your downfall. If you ever land a windfall of luck or circumstance, don't get lazy and quit doing what you should have been doing all along: taking action in a forward motion. So your best client gives you fifty percent more business this quarter than they did last quarter. Does that mean that you just stand there and enjoy the ride? So the economy sweetens the pot as far as the number of inbound calls you get for your product or service. Does that mean you forego your outbound marketing campaign? When life blesses you with fair winds and following seas, harness that energy to propel you swiftly to your goal.

Maybe your margins this year are better than last year. So are your competitors'. Just because the situations are promising doesn't mean it's time to get lazy. Remember that failure starts with success. Success can insulate us into a false sense of security in thinking that everything is comfortable, abundance abounds, and the harvest will always be plentiful. Symptoms of this disease of complacency are managers not training their people because 'we know everything,' companies not seeking new business when their funnels seem full, and organizations losing their edge because there's extra margin that can allow for sloppiness. Jim Rohn says that in the summer and fall when the seasons are still mild, the squirrel is always thinking, "Winter. . . winter. . . winter."

Here are three ways to overcome the tendency of complacency in your organization:

1. **Commit to getting an edge.** Remember that an edge, no matter how slight, is all you need to get ahead. Even if you work in a field that might not seem competitive, you are always competing against something. A few weeks ago I did a half-day workshop on partnering skills for a large MPI (Meeting Planners International) chapter convention. I told them that even though their jobs as meeting planners might not seem competitive in nature, they still have finite resources for which they must compete: time, energy, availability of volunteers, and budget limitations. When you think of your resources as being limited, then you become a good steward of them. You immediately eliminate sloppy business practices and get an edge when you start thinking this way. People only conserve that which they believe to be finite.
2. **Ask yourself: "Am I successful because of myself or in spite of myself?"** When we are honest with ourselves, then we always can see that we can get just a little bit better. Management consultant Alan Weiss calls this the 'One Percent Solution'. He says that if you just get better one percent every day, within a short period of time you'll be twice as good.

3. **Develop new habits as a team.** The power of a collective unit brings with it a strong advantage of synergy. When you start working together and everyone works on personal development, such as adopting the One Percent Solution, then the symbiotic and synergistic relationship in the team environment gets you that much further ahead. There is a direct impact on success that your team achieves when you build legitimate influence through authentic relationships. You can lead your team to try to develop these new habits together as a collective and unified force focused on a single success objective.

If you follow these steps you'll harvest more fruit and yield more success. But the best part of all is knowing that with every resource and every edge, you made the best of how you performed. And sometimes just knowing that you took full advantage of the advantage feels even better than winning.

CHAPTER 26
HOW TO INFLUENCE SELF-MOTIVATION

On a weekend when my son was three years old, we braved the cold and went to the park by the lake. We were the only kids at the playground, and although he had never felt comfortable with swings before, he decided to ride in one. I picked him up, put him in the junior version of a swing, the type with a complete seat and a chain on the front, and started pushing him. I pushed him for a few moments and then got in the big boy swing next to him and showed him how to make himself go back and forth without daddy's help. In just a few minutes, he learned how to create his own momentum by kicking his legs as he came forward, and bringing them back as he sailed backward. He was self-motivated, self-actualized, and having the time of his life.

My son learned that if he didn't keep up with the leg kicking action he would eventually come to a complete stop. He wasn't strong enough to create his own momentum, so I had to start pushing him to swing back and forth all over again. But once the momentum existed, all he had to do was maintain it. If there were not a consistent continuation of effort on his part, then the momentum of the swing would eventually wane to a complete stop.

Consider how your employees are dependent upon you as a leader to help them start the momentum of the energy of work.

You are responsible for initiating the momentum and transferring your energy to them. They depend upon you to lead them and to kick start the movement of the organization. Once the momentum is in place, all you need to do is give them the skills that they need to keep themselves going forward and keeping the energy in a constant state of flow. If the energy stops, then you must come in and restart that momentum all over again.

Here are three ways that you can help your staff become self-motivated to create their own energy:

1. **Be very clear on the direction of your organization and stick with it. Don't change plans too quickly.** Don't make each week a scattered melee of activity by your staff. I once conducted a leadership workshop in which part of the program included the attendees discussing past experiences of bad bosses. One of the attendees mentioned that he worked for

a manager who would change the strategy every two weeks. The team would get going in one direction, and then the plans would change. With managers who are without focus, or those who lead with an ever-changing focus, employees will eventually burn out and become apathetic. The energy of their movement will come to a complete stop with this type of leader.

2. **Remember that it's not about you. Your employees come to work for their own personal fulfillment, not for yours.** With each conscious attempt to use them to make yourself look better, you are taking away from that self-generated energy that is critical to keeping things going forward. Take your eyes off of yourself and fixate them squarely on the direction of the team and how you can serve your employees to manifest that vision. Ironically, by focusing on those two issues, the direction of the team and serving your staff, you will advance quicker in your career than by deliberately scheming to get ahead.

3. **Make sure they have the skills they need so that they can be successful and feel successful.** And when one of them hits a home run, share that with the rest of the group in public. Positive energy creates positive energy. It's up to you to add some every now and then by recognizing your employees.

Not only will you see your staff create their own self-generated energy, but they'll have more fun at work than a kid on a swing set.

CHAPTER 27
HOW TO EARN HIGH MARKS AS A LEADER

I once heard Joe Calloway use this exercise at a meeting to make this point:

If you could give yourself a grade as a leader, what would it be?

Consider three categories. First, grade yourself on how effective you think you are in leading your employees. Second, grade yourself on how effective you think you are compared to your colleagues. Third, grade yourself on your leadership effectiveness from the perspective of your employees. In other words, if they had to grade you, what grade would they give?

The first two grades you gave yourself are worthless and mean nothing. The only thing that counts is the grade that your staff would give you. It does not matter how good you think you are or how good you are compared to the other managers in your company. The only thing that counts in leadership is the ability to incite others to self-motivated actions that accomplish the mission of the team and elicit a response from them that is authentic, focused, and intentional.

To lead your staff, you must earn the right to lead them. Leadership is first taken, and then it's earned. Leadership is never given to you. Instead, you take it. You take it by adopting an attitude of leadership. You take it by living your life in a way that attracts both followers and greater levels of responsibility to you because of the type of person that you have become. Don't wait for someone to confer greater levels of leadership on you. By taking leadership you will eventually earn it. Even if you are currently absent of followers but want to grow in your career to greater levels of responsibility, you can start by leading yourself. Take ownership and total responsibility of your own personal outcomes. When you take full responsibility and actively seek out other areas to make the team better, to make yourself better, to make others better, then those who are looking to promote leadership talent will notice you. It is in your nature as a leader to want to raise the bar. You are taking leadership when you take responsibility.

Consider these three steps to adopting a leadership attitude:

1. **Start with an attitude of self-acceptance, self-discovery, and self-improvement.** The relationships that you have at work are not really that different than the relationships that you have with others in your life, such as your loved ones and your family. And to grow in those relationships you first start with the relationship that you have with yourself. Leadership is a relationship, and the first relationship is self-directed. By accepting full responsibility of how you live your life, you begin your path down the road of leadership authenticity. To change the direction of your life, your leadership effectiveness, you change your attitude.
2. **Sharpen your focus on the outcomes of the team.** What is it that we are trying to accomplish at work this month? That's the question you need to ask yourself and once you find the answer, share that with your employees. People need direction, and it's up to you to find that direction and communicate it to your teammates.
3. **You give up part of your control.** You cannot control the actions of your employees, so you might as well accept it. Instead, set up a direction of the team, clear expectations of what each of them needs to accomplish to reach their targets, and feedback systems that allow them to communicate concerns to you without fear and allow you to communicate guidance to them without guilt.

The title on your business card is a hollow shell if you can't back it up with congruence and leadership authenticity.

Forget about trying to influence others through your position of authority. Instead become the type of person that influences them with legitimacy and ignites their own self-motivated enthusiasm. And by following these steps, you will always earn high marks in the hearts of your employees.

CHAPTER 28
HOW TO FILL CRITICAL POSITIONS

One of my clients had difficulty finding a vice president to lead a new division of his company. This was a critical position, and not filling it grew into a critical problem. They were devoting a large amount of energy and commitment to developing a new niche, and each passing month without someone to run that new division meant that they were losing ground and market share.

"Scott, I am so frustrated," he told me. "By the time I find these rare candidates and get them to meet with me, they seem to lose interest in the opportunity and end up taking another position. How can I get them more excited about joining our company?"

We talked for a few moments about his hiring process, how he obtains new candidate resumes, and how he interviews them. "How much time goes by from the first time you read their resume to the time that you meet with them for the first interview?" I asked.

"Well, usually just a few weeks pass before I have time to meet with them. I travel a lot and my schedule is full."

"How many weeks is it then, on average?" I asked.

"Four, maybe five weeks. Sometimes six or seven," he responded.

"Let me ask you this, Steve. If your best client called you and told you that he needed you to fly to Chicago tomorrow, would you be able to make your client's request fit in your schedule?"

"Of course. I'd make the time. He's a client," he replied.

"Then you need to start treating your prospective employees like clients. What you're telling me is that you are frustrated because the candidates lose interest. What you are telling them through your actions is that they are not important to you because you take so long to move forward with them. I don't blame them for losing interest and exploring other opportunities. If you wait as long as two or three or four weeks to meet with a prospective employee, you are opening yourself up to variables beyond your control which can take the candidate out of the contention for the position."

I went on to share with him these three common pitfalls of most employers when it comes to securing talent for critical positions.

First, they delegate ownership of filling the position to another department like human resources. Human Resources may be good for broad sweeps of talent and routine hires, but for critical positions it is the line manager or department closest to that position who is the best source for securing the talent. Filling critical positions takes more than filling out a requisition form and submitting it to another department. Own it like any other critical project. Set target dates, scopes of responsibility, expectations from other parties involved, and action lists to find and acquire the talent.

Second, they lose momentum in the rhythm of the search. By treating your candidates like prospective clients you make them a priority. You should make first contact within twenty-four hours of seeing his or her resume. You should set up the first meeting within the next five business days. Schedule the second interview at the end of your first interview, and set it up within two to five business days and keep the flow of the search moving swiftly. Keep it moving forward with deliberation because you never know when your competitor will make an offer to the candidate.

Third, they don't understand that the hiring game is a relationship game. Relationships are built on frequency of contact. The more contact you have with the prospective candidate, the more of a relationship you are building. Just like developing a client, you want to engage in a series of positive meetings and interactions with the candidates through email, phone calls, letters, and meetings.

Make a commitment to avoid these pitfalls and see how much easier it is to acquire the best talent for your most important positions.

CHAPTER 29
HOW TO LISTEN WITH POSITIVE INFLUENCE

I only drink water without ice when I go to restaurants.

"What would you like to drink, sir?"

"Water, with no ice, please," I always respond to the waiter or waitress. Always.

And sure enough, forty percent of the time I get water with ice. I order it that way now just to test the wait staff and see what sort of a response I get. Then what's even worse is that I measure the response rate and keep a mental tabulation to see what sort of ratios I come up with. I can't help it. It's the curse of being a management consultant. I measure everything.

The way waiters and waitresses listen to my request is the same way that many of us listen to our employees. We kind of expect to know what the answer really is, but we rarely take time to think and just listen to what they have to say. We fail to empathize and instead anticipate what they are going to say because we think we already know what they want…so we give them water with ice when they asked for something else. We let our conditioned response get in the way of legitimate listening.

Here are three steps to increase your listening power the next time a co-worker or subordinate employee brings an issue to you:

1. **Sit down in chairs next to each other, not having a desk between you if possible.** Take your conversation away from the plant floor. By taking the time to sit, it sends a signal to your employee or colleague that they are important enough for you to dedicate a few moments just to them.
2. **Do NOT text or answer your phone while talking with your colleague.** Has this ever happened to you before when someone else answered the phone while talking with you? I was at the front desk of a hotel in Manhattan last week wanting to check in and go to bed and the clerk kept answering the phone and dealing with the callers when my issue wasn't being addressed. Here I am looking at the clerk three feet away from me talking on the phone. So I pull out my cell phone, call the front desk of the hotel, and the clerk answered. I said, "I'd like to check in to your hotel, please". He asked me when I would like to do this. I said, "Right now. I'm at your counter looking at you three feet away from you." It worked.

I now had his attention and checked in and went to bed. Don't let this great American habit of answering the phone or responding to texts while someone else is in front of you interrupt your time with your colleague.

3. **Empathize with what they're telling you.** Put yourself in their shoes so you understand their issue. Even if you disagree with them, people are usually okay with that as long as they are heard and as long as they are understood. This simple concept of empathy is the key to successful managing, leading, negotiating, and selling.

Bonus tip: Clarify your employee's issue by repeating it back in your own words and asking questions about it.

By following these simple steps, you are sure to hear what your colleagues and teammates are really telling you, and not just what you anticipate to hear. Now if only I had the time to teach this concept to every restaurant that I visit!

CHAPTER 30
INVESTING IN EMPLOYEES

Character development yields the greatest return on investment, and in corporate terms, that translates into leadership. Think about why people get fired. It rarely has to do with core competency issues of the tactical elements of job performance. Usually it is because of a character default, such as the inability to work with others, integrity issues, punctuality, and other areas that are frequently relegated to the "soft skills" sector of training. It is this critical skill set of leadership development that builds organizations.

If I owned a large company and was looking at where to put my investment dollars for my staff, I would help them become more effective leaders. Think about the best leader that you ever worked for. You would follow him or her anywhere. If he or she needed the team to put forth the extra effort, the team would double what he or she expected. That is the power of leadership. It has a significant economic impact on the bottom line. And leadership can be studied and brought into the workplace. Leaders should be developed at every level, and it is more than singing the company song or quoting the slogan of the week. It's about giving purpose to the lives of your team, and showing these team members how they can lead others and help others see how their daily tasks fit in with the long-term vision of the company.

What would leadership success look like if it could be measured? Anything that can be measured can be improved, and here are three key tangible ways to measure leadership effectiveness:

1. **What is the tenure within your company?** How long do people stay? Why do they leave? Ask any manager why someone leaves his or her department, and you'll rarely get the real answer. Because people don't want to give the real reason they leave. People join companies for professional reasons. They leave them for personal reasons. Leadership is a personal issue, and by becoming a better leader, you will become the employer of choice in retaining star talent.
2. **What is the attraction rate of your company?** What's your company's story? Why do people join the company? What are the values? What's the purpose? It's more than the strategic plan. Marines join the Marine Corps not because of a strategic plan, but because of pride and esprit de corps. If you grow in your leadership effectiveness and show others how

to do the same thing, you would be amazed to see how much pride is instilled in your workplace. This can only help when attracting your competitor's best people to your organization.
3. **What is the 'fun quotient?'** Mission accomplishment is critical, but having fun while doing it separates the star companies from their competitors. Do people have fun working in your company? By fostering an environment that opens up innovation and creativity, people are more inclined to enjoy what they do. And when they enjoy something, they will give their best effort. And the best effort is enough to give you an edge over your competitors. An edge, no matter how slight, is still an edge, and many times that's all it takes to win.

When you implement a leadership initiative, which is a focused effort on improving leadership skills within the company, it must be done with the right attitude. People observe leaders in their company to make sure they are congruent with the message they are sending. Any time there is a lack of congruence in developing leaders, it can do more harm than good for the organization. In other words, if an employee sees a manager lie to a client when he is telling his employees to be honest, then a negative deposit is put into the trust bank account with that employee. This distrust keeps building up more and more as employees witness similar experiences. If the initiative is implemented with sincerity, then the response is positive, as long as you show why you are doing the initiative. Tell your employees that leadership development programs are not just going to help the company achieve its goals, but that it will help the employees grow personally. People buy in to decisions that personally benefit them, so you need to show them what's in it for them when you implement such an initiative.

CHAPTER 31
AUTHENTICITY TO INFLUENCE SALES

A few years ago, I keynoted at a major California trade association convention in Los Angeles in the Hollywood area. I introduced the concept of integrating leadership principles into the sales process, and how today's sophisticated buyers are fed up with the selfish manipulations of traditional sales training. I explained the concept that a successful sales professional never has to say 'thank you' at the conclusion of the sale. If your value is high and your belief in your product or service is genuine, then it is the customer who should be saying 'thank you' to you. If you focus on creating and articulating the clear contribution of your value on a personal level to the end-user, then that prospect will eagerly make the investment in your product or service.

At the end of the convention, one of the board members came up to me and told me that the message resonated well in the hearts of the attendees, who were seasoned sales veterans. When I asked her why she thought the program was well-received, she said, "That's because this is Hollywood. We're so used to seeing fake and plastic people that any bit of authenticity is refreshing to us."

This is indeed an age of authenticity and congruence. People are tired of hype and are putting up impenetrable walls to keep marketers out.

Don't try to fight it. Go with it. Leverage this to your advantage in your sales process.

1. **Develop an insatiably high belief in the value of your product or service.** If you don't believe that there is a benefit to be realized to your customer from what you are selling, then you need to find something else to sell. Focus on contribution first, commission second.
2. **Get testimonial letters from your best clients.** Call them and ask them to give quantifiable representations of how your product or service has benefited them. Have them post these on LinkedIn. By showing specific benefits on a personal level that are quantifiable, you use the principle of social proof in why others should buy your product or service. The premise of this principle is that we make decisions to buy based on the decisions that others have already made. By making it quantifiable, it is irrefutable and much more compelling.

3. **Clarify your own personal values.** In your role as a business professional who wants to influence others, create a list of the three or four values or premises that govern your behavior. These should be the guiding force of all of your actions, including the sales of your products and services. Crystallizing your premises and beliefs gives you freedom to operate within that framework. You now have a reference point for your actions. This also increases your own personal self-confidence. By understanding who you are, what motivates you, and what governs your actions, you will start to perform at a peak level in your sales activities.
4. **When you have such a high belief in your own personal values and in the value of your product, then you now have a duty and a responsibility to overcome the prospect's objections.** If they give you an objection, your belief will be the main driving force of them purchasing your product, not your sales tactics. Most sales training is poor in teaching sales professionals how to properly sell, relying on gambits and manipulation more than authenticity and genuineness. It is the emotional belief in your contribution and the way that it will benefit them on a personal level that will encourage them to buy, not rebuttal number nine.

Integrate these influence principles into your sales process and watch how your prospects follow your lead. And at the end of the transaction they will thank you for your service to them.

CHAPTER 32
STRATEGIC INFLUENCE ON EMPLOYEES

"We're doing okay," he told me. "Everything's fine, so we don't need to fix anything. Our style of management is management by objective. We tell our people what to do, and they do it. We don't have any need to do leadership development."

"I understand, Bob," I replied. He was a third generation owner of a mid-sized general contractor, and the word on the street was that his turnover was high and morale was low. "But let me share this with you. I've learned over the years that those companies who became leaders in their field ended up that way by developing leaders in their own companies. You either grow or atrophy, and the growth of your company is directly related to the intentional development and growth of your people. Tell me how much time you spend developing your managers."

Silence on the phone. I rephrased the question.

"From zero to one hundred percent of your time, how much of it is spent developing the leadership and management skills of your managers?"

"I don't know. My direct reports handle that," he responded. I could tell by his hesitation that he didn't think the issue was important. He didn't consider leadership development to be a core competency of a business owner.

"So what exactly do they do to develop them and improve their leadership and management performance?" Silence again. "Bob, would you ever put your crews on the job site without giving them the right tools?"

"Of course not," he responded.

"So why are you doing that with your managers? You put them in the field and in the corporate office and tell them what to do, but you've never equipped them with the tools they need to lead their teams and manage their people effectively." I went on to explain how during Jack Welch's time as CEO of General Electric he spent forty percent of his time in a deliberate and focused effort to develop his people. And now his protégés are the most sought-after executives among the Fortune 500. In a similar way, Charles Krulak planned his days in advance to deliberately spend a third of his time face to face with his employees. Krulak was in charge of 5,000 employees at MBNA Europe, and is a former commandant of the Marine Corps. While serving as a young officer in Viet

Nam, he saw how face time with his troops helped develop them. He didn't even need to have a structured format. Time spent in the development of employees is well spent and always results in a visible return on investment.

But there is a problem with this type of thinking. It is strategic, and that's beyond the immediate scope of most managers and leaders. So much of the time spent by senior level managers is dedicated to reacting to the most immediate problem at hand, when it would be better invested in a strategic and deliberate way on those activities that would have kept the problems from surfacing in the first place. If you don't spend time brushing and flossing, you'll lose your teeth. If you don't spend time developing your employees, you'll lose your team.

Bob told me basically that he didn't have time to develop his people and that things were good enough and the conversation waned to a rough conclusion. The concept of strategic and deliberate growth and development of his staff was too far out, too far ahead of his immediate problems, and considered a waste of his time. Unfortunately, he'll end up continuing to react to crises and problems, trying to stop the leaks in his organization instead of trying to build a better dam.

In today's competitive market, good enough isn't good enough. You must continue to improve, and the best place to start is to improve the performance and leadership capabilities of your team. Good managers want to develop these skills. Remember that if you don't do it, your best competitors will.

CHAPTER 33
LEADERSHIP STYLES

What comes to your mind when you hear the word "leader"?

Do you remember the movie "Patton"? When you even think of that name, the image of an aggressive General Patton standing in front of the flag giving a memorable speech comes to your mind, right? Sure, that's what leadership is all about. Giving long speeches designed to inspire us, swearing profusely and strutting around with a chest full of medals. Well, that's not exactly the style of leadership that is appropriate for every person or every situation, but it's probably one style out of a hundred. Each style of leadership is as unique as every snowflake that falls, as unique as each one of us. It is this uniqueness that is both motivating and confusing as manager steps into a leadership role and tries to identify his or her leadership style.

Different styles are appropriate for different employees and different scenarios. As a manager discovers his or her own unique styles of leadership, he or she will then develop a sense for when to apply them. How to learn this can be done in the following three steps:

1. **Observe what is effective and what is not.** For a morning journaling exercise, write each morning for the next week on the past year of your life, specifically the experiences at work that resulted in positive outcomes with your team. Write down each event and outcome, who was involved, and how you would describe your leadership style. This gives you a baseline for your leadership style, and how malleable your methods have been. You can then develop a specific leadership system of how you personally manage your team. Next week, your exercise is to journal about every boss that you've ever had. Describe their style and its level of effectiveness on you as an employee and team member.
2. **Read on leadership daily.** The bookstore is filled with material on leadership. Leadership can be taught (or more specifically, it can be learned), and if we all figured it out by now, there wouldn't be any more books on leadership. Things haven't changed much since the Egyptians built the pyramids, and managers still face the exact same problems and scenarios that have been faced for thousands of years. Someone has probably experienced a situation similar to yours, and they've written about it. Be a student for your entire life on this important subject.

3. **Find a mentor.** If you want to go somewhere that you've never been to before, hire a guide to take you there. This could be an experienced executive within your company, a former professor of management from your school, or a paid executive coach or consultant. I personally believe that something this important requires a person who has a strong interest in seeing you develop as a leader.

Work on your style and be open to changing it as new and different scenarios reveal themselves in front of you. And hopefully your subordinates will have an inspiring memory of you in their minds when someone mentions the word "leader".

CHAPTER 34
LEADERSHIP BY QUESTION-ASKING

Once on a long cross-country flight, I boarded the plane with only one piece of luggage, one carry-on item, and one really bad attitude. And, as I sat back in my spine-pinching coach-class seat, I became even grumpier. I had rushed to the airport, skipped breakfast, didn't have time to get a muffin or even a necessary cup of coffee, almost missed my flight, and knew that my only food item was going to be bad airplane coffee and a bag of stale pretzels. I was less than an ideal customer.

The flight attendant intuitively knew I was in a bad mood. But she smiled pleasantly and asked, "Is there anything I can do to make your flight more pleasant?" "Grrrrrr...no, ma'am," I responded. Just feed me a real meal for a change and a decent cup of coffee, I thought to myself. But my hostility had been diffused by her polite professionalism. And I thought about the question she asked me: 'Is there anything I can do to make your flight more pleasant?' Now that's a good question. It focuses on the core competency of her job description: customer satisfaction. She just came right out and asked it.

A challenge for many managers is that they neglect the core competency of not just of their own positions, but the jobs of their subordinates. Who can blame them? It's a busy world with an incessant melee of competing time demands. There needs to be some simple and easy way to bring things back to focus and center on the core competency of the employee.

Here's a possible solution: today, when you see one of your employees or teammates on the floor, right smack in the middle of trying to finish a deadline, ask them this: "Is there anything I can do for you that can help you be more effective with what you're trying to do?"

It's a simple question, but it cuts right to the chase of what you are all about as a manager, and what they are all about as a member on your team. And it's a congruent question without a hidden agenda, without a "manager-centered" focus, and without hostility. It focuses on employee competence, employee satisfaction, manager competence, manager satisfaction, and outcome accomplishment. Just be sure to have a good breakfast and a cup of coffee before even thinking about asking management-related questions of your employees.

CHAPTER 35
POSITIVE INFLUENCE IN CRITICAL SITUATIONS

My son went to see his dentist, who was a bright young woman in her early thirties who seemed very dedicated to her profession and very sharp. She seemed very enthusiastic about her vocation, and in the course of our conversation I asked her why she became a dentist.

"I make an immediate impact on the health of my patients. It's significant, but it's also immediate. I was considering medical school, but as a doctor, it might take years to see the results in a patient. When they come to me as a dentist, they leave my office with their problem solved."

Perfect sense, I thought. And from that I learned an insight into why dentists become who they are, and stumbled upon another key motivation of employees.

Everyone wants to feel like they accomplished something, but sometimes it's tough to see exactly what that just might be, especially if it is a very large project or if a melee of activity clouds the focus in times of crisis. On most large company projects or processes, there might be fifty contributors to the final outcome, and many of those will never ever see the final desired event.

In the movie *Twelve O'clock High,* Gregory Peck plays the part of a squadron commander who assumes command of a failing squadron. His first instinct is to assume command with an iron fist, which was not at all a bad idea, since a previous commander who put personal preferences and personal issues ahead of critical mission issues had diluted leadership authority.

As Peck's role in the movie intensifies, he is given an assignment that might cause the loss of every life in his unit. So he begins talking about the mission to his men. He tells them about their small part in the whole scheme of things. He tells them that with their focus on mission accomplishment with this one particular mission, other units will follow in behind them to wipe out significant Nazi strongholds and win major battles that would tip the balance in favor of the allies. In other words, he tells them what the results of their efforts are going to be. Just like my son's dentist, they will know that there was a significant and positive impact, even though they might not live long enough to witness those final results. In the movie, they know that their efforts will not be in vain and that their small role is a critical link in the chain of intense progress.

All of us hate wasting our time. We cannot stand to think of working on a task that does not help us move forward in the accomplishment of a pre-determined outcome. Your employees are the same way. They yearn for success. They long to contribute. I believe that people really do want to do a good job. Every employee at some level wants to see the team win. No one wants to waste his or her time or work for an outcome that will never be considered productive.

Here are three action steps to keep in mind as you lead your team in critical times:

1. **State the vision.** Tell them where they are going and what the future will look like.
2. **Tell them what you need from each of them.** Be specific, and always link their role with the vision.
3. **Talk about the greater good.** It has to be more than profit margins and shareholder value. You need to have a win for the prospect, a win for the team, and a win for the greater good in general. It's easy when you make a product or provide a service that saves lives or positively impacts the health of someone. So for most of us, we have to stretch our narrative and articulate how all the dots are connected between our product and service and how it impacts the greater good

On my minesweeper, during Operation Desert Shield and Desert Storm, I read about the Iraqi invasion into Kuwait as it happened. I was the operations officer so I was in the communications room and my chief petty officer said, "Sir, looks like we are going to war." Our world changed overnight. A few weeks later, we were getting ready for our sea trials since our minesweeper was the next boat to rotate to the gulf.

We had problems with our sonar, and we needed to get it to work prior to our sea trials. If we didn't pass our sea trials, we wouldn't be ready to deploy. It was the fourth weekend in a row that the sonar technician, a twenty-year old second class petty officer, needed to stay aboard and work on the sonar. He had a young family and I knew he was feeling stress at work and stress at home.

I could use my authority and tell him that I am ordering him to give up another weekend to get the sonar fixed. Or I could try to influence him.

"Petty Officer Schaeffer, I need to talk to you in my stateroom." He walked in and uncovered (took off his cap) and stood there wondering what was up. "As you know, the Iraqis have invaded Kuwait. We have international support against them and this is what is called a classic 'just war'. The U. S. fleet needs to sail into the harbor but we can't reach them because of all of the mines. But if we can't get underway on Monday, then we miss our window and we can't accomplish the mission. Right now, this little minesweeper is the most important ship in the fleet. Right now, you are the most important sailor in the United States Navy. I know you have not been home on a weekend in four weeks, but I need for you to give it one more weekend and get the sonar working."

He stood there for a moment and took it all in. I didn't have to explain it to him that way. I could have used my position of authority to accomplish the objective. Instead, I influenced how he felt about accomplishing the job by connecting his work with the full impact of what we were trying to do.

Remember this, that people do not come to work every day for you. They come to work for themselves. You have to tie in their own personal goals and dreams and align those with the mission of your team, especially in critical situations. If you do this, you will earn a massive amount of loyalty in your efforts to positively influence them.

CHAPTER 36
THE PROBLEMS WITH COMMAND AND CONTROL

Years ago managers tried to institutionalize the concept of leading their teams, not even considering the emotional impact of their style. Perhaps this is because our traditional system of management is a derivative of the military style that was necessary to manage a crisis, the Second World War. In times of crisis, fast unquestioned orders are the most effective ways to lead. Combat is not a time to create focus groups or quality circles. This style is also known as "authoritarian" or "command and control" management.

But that same type of leadership was passed on to our developing economic system in the 1940's and 1950's and is a remnant in many organizations today. Most managers have never been to a leadership development program, have never read a leadership book and have never heard a leadership speaker. So they lead the way their boss led them, who led the way his boss led him, who led the way his boss led him, who ... and it results in a command and control organization at a time when the situation does not require it, and at a time when the cultural norms of our society reject it. Leadership with an authoritarian mindset causes employees to push back and put forth minimum effort, doing only what is barely required to keep from getting fired or punished. This style of leadership removes the manager from the emotional impact of the orders given, safely distant from the feelings that show up to work every day with the staff.

Managers wonder why there is bad morale, complacency, turnover, poor performance, and other problems in their company. The real problem is that most managers are unwilling to fix the real problem: how they lead. They refuse to change, to learn, to grow, and to develop themselves or their team leaders and instead criticize and complain about the performance of their staff. But both the problem and the solution start at the top, not the bottom. If there are management problems in your company, the resolution of them through leadership development lies squarely on the shoulders of the owner or the senior manager of the organization. There is no other person who is responsible for leadership development except for the captain of the ship.

A few years ago, I visited four partners of a bank in Manhattan. They first called me in because of sales-related issues. After ninety minutes of me asking questions I said, "Let me give you some tough love. Your problems have nothing to do with banking or business development activities. The problems that you face stem from not knowing how to lead on an emotional level." What I meant by that was this: They forgot how to empathize with the people in their company and with their customers. They had caught "CEO Disease." They had lost touch with the heart of their organization and were managing with command and control, far removed from the emotions in the company.

"Here's an example of how you've lost touch. Have you ever sat in the waiting area of your loan department? When I was waiting in your lobby, I observed the behaviors of those here to submit loan applications. The tension in the air was thick and they were all nervous, and your lobby does nothing to make the customer feel relaxed and comfortable. They don't care about your mission statement on the wall or your awards. They want to be comfortable and relaxed and you do nothing to help them feel this way." I showed them that if they were neglecting the emotional impact of their business on the customer, then they were more than likely neglecting the emotional impact on the employees.

Perhaps you are too close to your problems. Start leading on an authentic and emotional level, get rid of command and control, and see how many problems are solved just by developing the leadership skills within yourself and your staff.

CHAPTER 37
INFLUENCING IN TIMES OF CHAOS

You've just been promoted to a new department and have to get up to speed quickly. How can you assess the history, current situation, challenges, and strategic direction of an organization in a short period of time and cope with it all? Or perhaps your best customer has just made a huge deviation from their normal pattern of orders and it's going to take some maneuvering to get everyone else in the company to increase capacity or modify the specs of the original product design. You've never experienced anything like this before and you only have a short period of time to take action. Welcome to chaos. So how do you manage it?

Change within your organization is non-stop and its ensuing byproduct is the unknown. The quicker we can get a handle on the situation, the sooner we can bounce back to a state of confidence and a command of the situation and start feeling like we have a clue again. Resilience is a core competency of strong managers and high performing sales people.

In the martial arts, your stance gives you power and a position of advantage over your opponent. When it comes to winning in a competitive market, managers who learn how to stand on solid ground operate from a position of power and a sense of control over those circumstances.

There are five steps that the resilient manager must follow to quickly recover to a position of strength:

1. Assess the situation.
2. Assess the options.
3. Get input from smart and knowledgeable people.
4. Determine a direction and make decisions.
5. Execute.

Recovery is actually quite simple as long as you know which questions to ask and how to think. Follow this line of questioning to help you quickly get a grip on the situation:

Who, What, When, Where, Why and How.

Here are a few examples of how these short and simple phrases can be integrated into tools of analysis. Don't let the simplicity of this line of questioning keep you from using it. Try it out and see if it works for you.

Who are the players associated with this new development? Who do I need to have on my team who are not already on it?

What steps have been taken so far?
What steps need to be taken in the next two weeks?
When did this change occur?
When are the deadlines associated with action items that I need to take?
Where did the change feel the biggest impact?
Where do I need to spend my time?
Why did my client change their order?
Why did my staff respond this way?
How did this affect my relationship with my client?
How do I need to manage that relationship?

You get the picture. When we start using basic principles of analysis, we can start thinking critically and asking those questions that eventually lead to the information and ideas needed for recovery. If you need to, write the W5H questions on a single sheet of paper with a few spaces between the six words. You'll figure out which specific questions to ask as you start investigating your situation.

Here are a few words of caution: Spend thirty percent of your time in the analysis portion of your job and seventy percent in the actions. That's thirty percent going over steps one through four, seventy percent on step five, which is to execute. It is your action that gives you momentum, power, velocity, and traction. When you step forward with your left foot, right foot, left foot, right foot, you are going forward and you still have time to think while you are moving ahead.

When you have nearly all the facts, then that's enough. You don't need to know everything. In a fast-paced world, sometimes you have to live in the land of 'good enough'. And when it comes to resilience, action is the balm that soothes the wounds of chaos.

CHAPTER 38

MISSION ACCOMPLISHMENT

Several years ago *The Wall Street Journal* ran an article about a progressive way to fill open billets for the U. S. Navy. It's through an online bidding system similar to EBay. It pairs up motivated sailors who desire to live in obscure locations with open billets. For example, it fills a billet in an otherwise undesirable location in Italy with a sailor who is married to an Italian citizen. The concept seems to be both congruent and effective and it accomplishes the mission of filling open positions with those qualified and geographically motivated sailors who have the highest likelihood of benefiting the most. The end of article trailed with an anticlimactic quote from a Commander saying that this method of filling open billets was an absurd system of weakness and diminished our Navy's quest for sea power.

Perhaps this officer thought that trying to serve the needs of subordinate employees was a sign of weakness. I found his comments ironic because the first leadership lesson taught to midshipmen at Annapolis is that leadership in its purest form is servanthood. It was a lesson that we learned on our very first day as plebes and heard about every day until we threw our hats in the air four years later: Take care of your people. Take care of your people. Take care of your people.

But how does a manager or an entrepreneur balance the needs of the mission with the needs of the employees? How can you accomplish the mission when so much of your energy is focused on taking care of your people?

I asked that question to Walt Boomer, the former CEO of Rogers Corporation in Connecticut. Rogers is a high tech foam company that sustained significant and real growth under Boomer's leadership. In the military he retired as a general wearing four stars on his lapel, serving as the Assistant Commandant of the United States Marine Corps. If anyone could help me to understand the dichotomy and balance, it would be him.

"Walt," I asked, "What's more important: taking care of your people? Or mission accomplishment?

He paused with careful thought and said, "Taking care of your people, Scott. Definitely taking care of your people. If you have the right people in place and if you take care of them, they will accomplish the mission."

In General Boomer's simple response hides the secret of successful organizational development. First, build your team with the right people and only the right people.

Second, get real clear with them on the mission. Third, take care of them. And that's it. Real simple.

But here's the breakdown in most organizations. First, the wrong people are on the team. Second, they don't understand the mission. Third, most managers are too preoccupied with protecting their own self-interests that they perceive the needs of their people to be a sign of weakness as a manager. And that's it. Real simple.

Here are three steps to bring your focus back to authentic leadership without losing mission focus:

1. **Develop a strategy of hiring the best of breed and putting only the best talent in those positions.** This is a core competency and deserves the priority focus of line managers. Most organizations place hiring on the back burner because they have the false notion that it is far removed from cash flow and revenue generation. Train your managers on how to hire the best performers, not the best interviewers.
2. **Make sure each employee has a clear understanding of the mission of the organization.**
3. **Develop systems to ensure that your team measures up to the reality of expectations, not your perceptions.** What is worse than having the wrong people in place is keeping the wrong people in place?

If you follow these steps and keep your focus on authentic leadership, you will build strength of leadership and find that mission accomplishment is easier to achieve with a willing and motivated team.

Printed in Great Britain
by Amazon